Financial Lovemaking 101

Merging assets with your partner in ways that feel good

Blue Boy Publishing Company

Blue Boy Books are published by The Blue Boy Publishing Company, 23F Queens Way, Camillus, NY. 13031

Printed in the United States of America.

First printing: January 2006
10 9 8 7 6 5 4 3 2 1

Cover design by Andrea M. Hatter

Disclaimer

This book is designed to provide education and general information in the areas of relationships and financial management. Laws vary from state to state, and are subject to change. The reader is therefore advised to seek individual consultation during the implementation of this advice.

The author has taken all meaningful and reasonable precautions to ensure the accuracy of the material presented in this book as of the date it was written. Neither the author nor the publisher assume responsibility for the errors or omissions which may occur in this text. The author and publisher disclaim any liability resulting from the use or application of information in this book, and the information is NOT intended to be used as legal advice for individual or group situations.

To Leah,

Bless you.

Special Thanks and acknowledgements

I would like to give thanks to Romana Lavalas for amazing support during the editorial process. I would like to thank Lawrence Watkins, my business manager, for providing invaluable loyalty. Andrea Hatter did a wonderful job designing the cover. I would also like to thank: Amani Herron, Robin Watkins, Dorian Chandler, Lakisha Clark, Michael Eric Dyson, Marc Lamont Hill, Larry Watkins, Diana Atkinson, and others who were instrumental in the completion of this project.

I would also like to pay tribute to the millions of Americans who have supported me along the way. The journey has been challenging, but without my fans, I would be nothing.

Sincerely,

Dr. Boyce D. Watkins
"The People's Scholar"
www.financiallovemaking.com
To contact about speaking engagements, please call (502) 640-8155

Financial Lovemaking 101

Merging assets with your partner in ways that feel good

Dr. Boyce Watkins

www.FinancialLovemaking.com
www.MyFinanceProfessor.com
www.BoyceWatkins.com

BLUE BOY PUBLISHING

TABLE OF CONTENTS

Disagreements over money are the number one problem for couples in America[1]

Love is a beautiful thing. One of the most beautiful and powerful experiences a human being can imagine, and also one of the most painful. Love can make you fly through the air like a crack head on payday, or it can have you running down the street in your underwear screaming satanic phrases. It has a powerful impact on the mind, one that is both exhilarating and devastating. There usually is no in-between, at least not at first.

I've been in love. I've fallen out of love. I've fallen back in love again, and then climbed back out. Sometimes I was thrown out, and sometimes I was spat out. No matter how I entered love or found myself out of love again, I wouldn't trade those experiences for the world. Love truly makes the world go round, and making love is one of the most` natural things a human being can do with another.

What exactly does it mean to "make love"? Is it like baking a cake, or making a costume? Is it the creation of something where there was nothing there before? Perhaps I should stop being so damn philosophical, but then again, that is what love makes you do. It turns a prostitute into a Plato, a journeyman into a genius. It makes us sometimes pretend to be something

[1] Council of Relationship study, 2006

we're not, and it can unleash that part of us which was dormant in the first place.

One thing I've learned during all these conversations is that money is *not* everything. In fact, if money and lovemaking were on a menu right next to one another, I would certainly choose to be a smiling man with empty pockets.

As a full time finance professor and full time geek, I have also thought about the love making process. Not just the ins and outs of it all, but I've also thought about love making as it relates to sharing money.

I'm an honest person, and I talk about honest things. This book discusses money, love, sex and everything in between in a realistic, yet silly and fun-loving way. Sex is one of the most natural things a human being can experience, and there is no shame in it. I think it's okay to talk about oral sex, sex in public places, orgasms, and all the other things that the birds and the bees do. Making love is a beautiful process, and I am not sure who decided that sex should be an evil or taboo topic, especially since most people think about it with more frequency than they'd care to admit.

Money is also a taboo topic for many people. They shy away from talking about it, lie about it, manipulate one another because of it, and even kill over it. We are told not to ask people how much they earn, how much they are worth, how much they have invested or how much they have saved. Even in the midst of relationships, one partner may not feel comfortable talking about money with the other. For some reason, someone decided that money and love don't mix. But I would argue that money and love are more intimately related than most realize. And it is this intimacy which this book seeks to explore.

This book is going to teach you how to make love. Not physical love, for that is another book. It teaches you the art of financial love, which can be just as fulfilling, just as frightening, just as dirty and just as thrilling as its physical counterpart. I call this concept, "Financial Lovemaking." That is, merging your assets with your partner ways that feel good.

Financial Lovemaking is about loving your partner enough to invite harmony into your financial relationship. It is about studying one another's spending, saving and investing habits to ensure that there is going to be harmony in your relationship. It means that you know how to look out for warning signs and work through them. It also teaches you when it might be best to walk away. It is always important to remember that loving someone is not the same as *living* with them, and if you can't live with them, then you may die a financial death with them in the end.

This book not only teaches you have to love your partner financially, it also teaches you how to love *yourself.* It's going to teach you how to make financial love in a way that builds your relationship to the heights you both expect. Both partners must come to the table with something to give, especially if each hopes to receive something in return. This is what makes love into what it is: an intimate partnership between two parties.

Bad Financial Lovemaking can be worse than bad sex: it can be driven by selfishness, deceit, gluttony or manipulation. As in a sexual relationship, a financially intimate relationship is no place to put misguided trust, because bad financial and sexual choices can ruin your life. This book will teach you how to enjoy this process for what it's meant to be: something that takes you to financial climaxes you couldn't reach on your own, and draws you closer to your partner.

As a Finance Professor, I am going to teach you many of the principles I have shared with students while teaching Financial Planning at the college level for the past 13 years. I am going to explain them in a way that allows you to see financial planning as an intimate process, one that blends with the rest of your life choices. I am also going to allow you to see how it can impact other aspects of your life in both positive and negative ways.

Our country obsesses over money, the same way it obsesses over sex. I personally don't believe that money is everything. Again, if choosing between money and love, I would choose love every time. But then again, why should it be one or the other? These choices don't have to be distinct. You don't have to choose love over money (or vice versa). This book will help you understand that if you are choosing in the right way, making the right financial decisions also increases the amount of love available to you in the end.

FINANCIAL SEX EDUCATION

GETTING FAMILIAR WITH THE FINANCIAL LOVEMAKING PROCESS

More than three-quarters of young couples divorcing before age 30 reported financial problems as the primary cause of their divorce. Another study found one-third of married couples cited money as their #1 issue[2]

[2] Rosanne Farnden Lyster and Jane Olsen - http://www.bccf.bc.ca/couplemoney.htm

When I teach Finance to college students, I come into class and ask them all the same question: "How many of you in this room have a portfolio?" Of course, with the students only being 21 years old and younger, nearly all of them keep their hands down. I am sure that many of their parents have investments in stocks, bonds and real estate, but many of my students haven't invested in much of anything yet, other than extra kegs of beer, sorority sweatshirts, and trips to the movies with the girl down the hall. I am sure that my question leaves them confused and thinking that I just got off the "Stupid Truck" that morning.

I then turn to one of the students in the front row and ask, "Did you come to class naked?" Of course, this question draws a laugh. As the student responds that he obviously did not come to class naked, I then ask the class whether their clothes cost money. They answer, "Yes". I ask them whether they could sell their clothes, their stereos, or their books for money right now, and they all agree that they could. Through this series of questions and answers, I explain that they do indeed have a portfolio of financial assets, and they are getting a return on their investment. It just happens that their return consists of something other than money. By "return on an investment", I am referring to anything you get back for the funds you have put aside. For example, if you buy a home for $100,000 and sell it for $132,000, some would say that your return on investment was $32,000. But what is important about return is that it doesn't always consist of money. Some people would own a home even if the value didn't increase over time. This could be because they are getting something back for their investment that is non-financial. I will define "return on investment" again in the next paragraph so that we understand each other.

A “financial asset” is something of value that you own. It can be stocks, bonds, or a pair of sneakers. A “portfolio of assets” is a **collection** of valuable items. It can be a set of stocks, bonds and real estate, or it can be your shoes, dresses and stereo. A “return on an investment” means that you spent one thing to get another. It can mean that you paid cash for a stock and earned more cash in return, or that you invested your energy into a relationship and the relationship grew stronger. The terms “portfolio”, “asset” and “return on investment” don’t just relate to money….they relate to life.

My explanations don’t always make sense to the students, because most people think of a portfolio as a collection of financial investments, like stocks, bonds, race horses or singing chickens. But clothing, stereos and even kegs of beer can be considered part of a person’s portfolio of assets. The difference is that rather than getting money out of the investment, he is getting something else of value. The valuable return might be the high from getting drunk, the thrill of wearing a new outfit or the pleasure from purchasing a new pair of shoes. My lesson to the students is very simple: money is not the only thing you get from an investment.

If money were the only thing you could get from an investment, then there would no reason to invest in our children. Children don’t usually give back the money that was spent raising them. They just show up with their hands out, like little welfare recipients. While it might make you want to shake them, you knew what you were getting into when you decided to give birth to them. But something inside of you says it’s okay to invest in your kids, even when you aren’t getting anything financial in return. That is because, psychologically, you are getting a return on your investment, but without money. That is because the return on your investment is psychological, not financial.

Next, I ask my students about "investments." I simply ask "What is an investment?" Usually, the finance majors in my class will say something like "It's when you put money into something to get more money back out." I then explain that, according to this definition, a person who does not have money can't make an investment. Further, this definition implies that the only valuable resource in the world is MONEY. That would mean that before there was money, there was nothing in the world of value. But of course, that isn't true. Before there was a common currency, people traded horses, chickens, labor, even their bodies, to get what they needed.

My point to the students is that money is only one type of investment. It is also only one type of wealth. Our most valuable assets are usually non-financial. Examples might be our time, our energy, or our love. A person can make an investment without money ever becoming a consideration. Not understanding the value of your non-financial assets can make you feel poor when you are actually quite wealthy.

Understanding the importance of intangible assets, such as our time, our health, or our love, is the way a person can find out how truly wealthy they actually are. One can also understand their own choices and behavior in order to figure out why they make investments that don't seem to make any sense. For example, why would you pass up on the chance to make money in order to go to your child's soccer game, or to call your mother and tell her how much you love her? Some might say these choices do not represent true investments, but I disagree.

Remember, an investment is the allocation of scarce and valuable resources toward a purpose that adds additional value in the future. *Hence, even the decision to stay home and do nothing is an investment.* In this case, the investment is your free time, and the return on the investment might be well-needed rest, which is important for your physical health. A person who takes a lower-paying job that gives him more time to spend with his family is also making an investment, since his return is going to be non-financial. Only seeing the financial output on an investment is like looking at a buffet with 200 courses, and only trying the carrots.

There are other financial concepts that we professors teach, such as "diversification" and "the relationship between risk and return." Finance professors make these concepts confusing, but I argue that we have intuitively understood these concepts our entire lives. "Diversification" is basically defined as not "putting all your eggs into one basket." So, if you own stocks, you should have several stocks, so that if one goes down, another goes up to balance it out. Most of us have known our entire lives that you should not "put all your eggs in one basket." The "risk return relationship" demonstrates that when an activity involves a higher level of risk, we need a higher reward for engaging in it. So, if someone says "Go run down the street naked", you are going to say "no". But if he offers you a million dollars to do it, your response might be "So, how far do I have to run?" You have basically done the trade off between risk and return in your head, and decided that the risk of being naked might be worth it for a million dollars.

Remember: a portfolio is a collection of valuable assets that you own. But, when you think about the word "portfolio", I no longer want you to think financially. Of course money is valuable, and it can be part of your portfolio, but I want you to think about the other aspects of your life that are more valuable than money, like your time, your relationships with loved ones, your energy level, physical health, love, etc. These, intangible items are also part of your portfolio.

One hard and fast rule of investing is that you should never change any part of your portfolio without considering how that change is going to affect the other parts. For example, if you get an offer for a new job with a 20% raise, would you take the job if it meant that you were going to have to move to Timbuktu and never see your family again? Probably not! What you have effectively done is decided that an increase in the financial side of your portfolio is not worth potential damage to the emotional side of your portfolio. There are many things of value that don't relate to money. THAT is how you should think about money and investing.

Many times, when I talk about portfolios, wealth and investing, I am talking about LOVE. Money is still important, but rather than money being the end result of your investment strategy, it can also be considered to be a tool for the enhancement of your love relationships. Also, I present methods to help you keep from allowing money to destroy the love that is in your life. Love is one of the most valuable assets in our life portfolio. Mismanaging the love side of your portfolio by allowing money to ruin it can literally destroy your life. You've heard people say things like "Love matters more than money". Well, they're right, it does. But what they fail to mention is that if you don't manage your financial relationship with another person, it can literally ruin the love you have for one another. Millions of divorces occur because of financial problems. I have seen spouses commit suicide over the financial devastation in their marriage, fathers walk out of the home, and women and men go to jail during divorce. Money almost always gives you yet another reason to fight with your partner. The problems can run from the mundane to the extravagant. I have seen couples fight because one partner makes more money than the other and believes that the income disparity entitles him to more power in the relationship. I have seen families destroyed because one partner took the money out of the family bank account and lost it at the casino. Your partner's bad financial habits can ruin your life. Here is just a small list of ways that someone could ruin your life financially:

- *A partner with horrible credit could keep you from ever getting loan.*
- *A partner with terrible spending habits can ruin a family's financial security.*
- *A partner with a substance abuse or other costly addiction could deplete a family's assets.*
- *A partner with unhealthy connections to deadbeat relatives, who always need money, may drain your assets.*
- *A partner with an income that is too low due to a lack of education or poor professional choices could ruin you financially.*
- *A partner may steal money from you or borrow it without your permission and use it for something frivolous.*
- *A partner who makes bad financial choices may get you into trouble with the IRS.*
- *A partner who decides to separate from you may end up dragging you and your money through a long legal battle.*

And, this is just the short list! As unromantic as it may sound, your Financial Lovemaking process is as important as the physical love you make, because it too, has deep and far-reaching consequences for your everyday life. This is the person you must live with for the rest of your life, so when the romance is gone and you are dealing with day-to-day activities, you may find yourself wondering how you made the bed in which you sleep every night.

SEX IS MONEY AND MONEY IS SEX

Twenty percent of women in committed relationships suspect that their partners have lied about finances; 16 percent of men in committed relationships feel the same way.[3]

[3] http://family-law.lawyers.com/Stats-and-Facts-Love-and-Money.html

The first thing I should say about the Financial Lovemaking process is that there is a difference between respecting the importance of money, and obsessing over money. Many people in American society simply dig for gold in their partners, and leave everything else behind. These people have "married for money" and are focusing on only one dimension of their portfolio, ignoring all the others. These individuals usually end up miserable. An example might be the woman who has decided to marry a multimillion dollar NFL star for his money, but as a result must contend with her husband's 14 girlfriends spread out around the country. This is not meant to indict all professional athletes, but you get the point.

Financial Lovemaking is not about making love to your finances. It's about making love to your partner while using your assets as financial foreplay (doesn't that sound kinky?). If done well, Financial Lovemaking can lead to satisfaction for both parties, better any sex toy you can imagine.

By now you're thinking, Okay, Dr. Watkins, how is Financial Lovemaking similar to good old fashion sex? Well, there are commonalties between physical and Financial Lovemaking, and I will cover them one by one.

- **(FINANCIAL SEX COMPARISON #1) YOU COULD DO IT BY YOURSELF IF YOU REALLY WANTED TO**

No one says that you have to merge your money or your body with another person's. There is a word we use to describe when someone takes care of his physical needs on his own, and I'm not afraid to say it. The word is "masturbation". Dr. Ruth told me a long time ago that the word is more of a gift to mankind than a sin. But then again, I'm not a priest.
Just as you can take care of your physical needs yourself, the same is true of your financial needs. There's an old saying "I can be broke all by myself." Thus, the decision to merge finances with another human being is not one we *must* make. Merging assets with another person is not a decision that should be taken lightly. It's a decision you make only if you see potential benefits from the interaction.

The benefits of making financial love should come in the form of increased family wealth (financial and non-financial), primarily due to financial synergies. Financial synergies refer to the added value of coming together, as opposed to two individuals doing something separately. In other words, "two plus two equals five". An example might be two people getting married, with each of them earning $50,000 per year. Their combined income is $100,000, but there are additional benefits. Not only has their income doubled, but because they are living together, their expenses have declined. Another example might be James and Tiffany, each of whom earns $50,000 per year. But instead of getting married and both working, they decide that Tiffany is going to work and James is going to stay home with the children. This saves money on daycare, and although average income has declined, there are still portfolio increasing benefits. First, the children are going to spend more time with their father. Secondly, Tiffany will be able to do a better job at work because she has someone handling the distractions at home. This may lead to additional career advancement opportunities. So, Financial Lovemaking synergies can add wealth, even if average incomes have actually declined.

- **(FINANCIAL SEX COMPARISON #2) IT'S ONLY FUN TO SHARE THE EXPERIENCE WITH SOMEONE WHO'S GOOD AT IT.**

A lot of people think that financial management is about expertise. They think that if a person has a high academic and financial IQ, he is going to be a good money manager. This is FALSE. Saving is like dieting: if you really want to do it, you don't have to be a nutritionist; you just have eat less junk food and take your fat butt to the gym. Similarly, in order to save, you have to make the decision to put money aside and reduce your spending. It's really that simple.

Making financial love with someone who is not good at it can be a horrible experience. Imagine having sex with someone who has no idea what he's doing. He could be selfish, prudish, abusive or manipulative. This individual is not someone you would ever sleep with again, and certainly not someone with whom you would want to share your life. Well making financial love with someone who doesn't know how to engage in the give and take of the Financial Lovemaking process can be equally horrific: that person may be greedy, wasteful, selfish or deceitful. This is not a person with whom you want to make financial love.

Finding out whether you are financially compatible with another person can either make or break your relationship. I provide information in this book on how you can go through this process, and also my website www.FinancialLovemaking.com allows you to read even more. If you and your partner aren't financially compatible, you might want to reconsider whether you want to merge assets with each other.

- **(FINANCIAL SEX COMPARISON #3) IT'S ONLY SAFE AND FUN TO DO WITH SOMEONE WHO HAS YOUR BEST INTERESTS AT HEART**

Making financial or physical love with someone who does not have your best interest at heart can lead to a horrible experience. The same way you wouldn't want to sleep with someone who has a sexually transmitted disease, you wouldn't want to merge assets with someone who has bad financial health. If your partner has bad credit, wastes money, or engages in practices that lead to a deterioration of his finances, then his bad financial health will inevitably destroy yours.

Many of us know what it's like to be rejected by someone we care about. Perhaps you have felt the effects other people's selfishness in your own life Good sex doesn't occur if one participant only thinks about satisfying his own needs. The same is true about Financial Lovemaking.

A person who has his own interest at heart is not interested in the idea of co-building assets. Such a person is usually only interested in building his own financial success, while using your wealth as a stepping stone. He spends your money freely, while hoarding his own. She is quick to drain your resources, while expecting you to keep her full. You can see very clearly how this is not as much a financial phenomenon as an emotional one. Bad outcomes sometimes involve one partner using the other, rather than sharing with the other. While one person is getting ahead, the other is being abused. Even without money in this equation, someone is being treated poorly.

Those who are sexually selfish often leave their partners physically and often emotionally unfulfilled. The same can be said of the financially selfish. A partner who hoards all his wealth while depleting yours doesn't see the value of financially contributing to the whole. This can leave you, with a financial and emotional deficit.

- **(FINANCIAL SEX COMPARISON #4) YOU MUST TRUST YOUR PARTNER**

If you don't trust your partner, the process of making love can have devastating consequences. In a sexual relationship, a partner who is not worthy of trust may betray us, or hurt us both physically and emotionally. This is the reason that an emotionally intelligent person spends time thinking carefully about the person with whom he will share his financial and physical assets.

I have regularly interacted with individuals who have fallen victim to trusting the wrong person. They find themselves in divorce court, losing half their wealth, after wasting half their lives. Individuals may also find themselves the victims of an IRS audit because their now ex-spouses left a pile of tax bills that he or she knew nothing about. Trust is as critical in the Financial Lovemaking process, as it is in the physical lovemaking process, and if you don't feel that you can trust your partner completely, you are probably better off without him/her.

Personally, I feel that trust takes time, and lots of communication. You should analyze not just what a person says, but what he does. This might mean observing a person's spending and saving habits, or taking notice of how much extra money he seems to have at any given point in time. You may also have to do an independent background check of some sort. Of course, the need for an independent background check implies a couple of negative things about your relationship: first, it implies that there is not enough trust in your relationship for you to ask your partner for the information directly. Second, it implies that you are contributing to the distrust by doing something without partner's knowledge. So, there is a continuous analogy between the physical and the financial. The same emotions on display when there is physical or emotional betrayal are in effect when there is financial betrayal. There really is not much difference.

- **(FINANCIAL SEX COMPARISON #5) EACH PARTNER MUST BRING SOMETHING GOOD TO THE TABLE IN ORDER FOR THE EXPERIENCE TO BE ENJOYABLE**

As in physical sex, financial sex can be terrible if your partner isn't bringing anything good to the table. Physical sex (for some) implies that the individual with whom you are sharing your body must be attractive to you in some way, and some would even argue, bring specific skills with him or her to enhance the quality of your love making process.

The necessary pieces of good financial and physical love depend on the situation and one's particular needs. Some prefer that their Financial Lovemaking partner bring a certain degree of "endowment" (a large endowment means you have a large amount of financial resources. A "well endowed" individual might be more enjoyable for a number of reasons that I won't necessarily go into right now) with them. Of course, a strong financial endowment can reduce financial problems in a relationship. While money doesn't necessarily buy happiness, I would argue that a lack of money gives you just one more thing to argue about.

Also, given that financial prosperity is one of the key objectives of nearly every American family, life is much easier when your partner can immediately contribute substantial wealth to the wealth building process. All else equal, it is usually easier to get along with a "good person" who is financially secure, than another "good person" who is not.

The down side to having a well-endowed partner is the risk that money can become an obsession. Things like prenuptial agreements, tax complications and emotional domination can become an issue. There are some couples who would much rather start off poor together than to have one partner possess a far greater amount of financial resources than the other. This imbalance can create challenges in a relationship.

Of course, as in physical sex, there are other pros and cons to having a well-endowed partner, since they say that "it's not the size of the ship, it's the motion of the ocean". So, perhaps it's not the size of someone's wallet that makes Financial Lovemaking enjoyable, it's the way they manage the finances they have available. The ability to get maximal enjoyment out of minimal resources is an important part of managing money. If an individual is well-endowed, but not careful with her money, she is always going to have one financial problem or another. There may be cash flow and liquidity problems, tax problems, problems managing investments, and the continuous risk that she is going to lose all the wealth in her possession. This threat would concern any reasonable partner, as this could affect the well-being of the entire family. Therefore, as part of your Financial Lovemaking, you are going to want to bond with someone who not only has something to work with, but they know how to work with what they've got!

(FINANCIAL SEX COMPARISON #6) YOU CAN GET BURNED IF YOU ARE NOT CAREFUL

I have heard story after story of someone who fell in financial love (or partnered) with the wrong person, and ended up regretting it for the rest of their life. This might come from a bad financial relationship with a mate, a business partner or a relative. The consequences can be devastating.

John's mother had become suicidal, in part because her husband had so much financial control over her. Her husband was an aspiring dentist when they met, and she was a sophomore in college. With her husband going into dentistry, she figured that she didn't have to worry about finishing her own education. So, she dropped out of school and depended on his income to support their family. I am sure you can predict the rest of the story. Twenty years went by, and they had 3 children together. They lived the American dream, with a home in the suburbs, a boat, two cars, and both of their children in private school. Then, when they were in their mid 40s, her husband informed her that he was leaving her for his secretary, a 22 year old woman.

As a result of her husband leaving, John's mother found herself in dire straits. She had to take her children out of private school and move into a 2 bedroom apartment. Her husband's attorneys were delaying any child support or alimony payments, so her income was essentially non-existent. Additionally, she was suffering the consequences of choosing to drop out of school to support his career in dentistry. She eventually attempted suicide. Fortunately, she recovered emotionally (on some levels), but never recovered financially.

The story of John's mother is an example of how risk in Financial Lovemaking can be tremendous. There must not only be tremendous trust, but there are times when we must protect ourselves even from those who truly love us. There are also times when we must protect ourselves *from ourselves.* That is the tricky part. This example also reflects the fact that making good financial love to someone else requires that we love OURSELVES. Love for yourself implies that you are making healthy choices, and that you have healthy expectations for your partner. It means that you are approaching your financial realities with a sense of maturity and focus on creating positive long-term results, and are therefore not in the business of enabling negative behavior on the part of your love partner. Additionally, it means that you are not expecting your partner to compensate for bad habits you choose to embrace. Below, we get into more detail regarding exactly how to make these decisions the right way, but for now, it is important to understand the big picture. There are many ways to be intimate, and many of them involve the dollar bill.

(FINANCIAL SEX COMPARISON #7) CHEATING CAN BE DEVASTATING

In physical lovemaking, fidelity is essential. Sexual cheating often leads to feelings of betrayal, but in this day and age, it can also lead to a funeral. There are sexually transmitted diseases today that didn't exist 20 years ago, and those who spend their free time cheating on their partner sometimes find that they've not only brought pain and hurt, but also a disease home to their own family. Another reality, however, is that some degree of infidelity is present in many, if not most relationships at some point in time. My goal is not to judge your degree of infidelity, but to talk about how to manage it.

Financial infidelity is similar to sexual infidelity. Financial infidelity may involve someone engaging in financial transactions without the knowledge of their partner. The consequences can be devastating. Examples might include supporting a gambling addiction, risky investments in the stock market (i.e. heavy use of options or futures without meaningful purpose), or other activities that are detrimental to your financial future. Cheating can be devastating in both physical and financial love, and the damage may be irreversible.

What's worse about cheating is that many times, the other partner has no idea that it's going on. Their trust has blinded them to the possibility that their partner might be hurting them or lying to them. They find out years later that their child's college fund has been depleted, or are shocked to find that the IRA plan has not been receiving the expected contributions each year. This signifies the importance of remaining financially empowered in your relationship, not to the point of being dominant, but to the point of receiving the respect you deserve.

You can protect yourself from cheating, first and foremost, by asking questions. Many relationships have a silent partner, which is almost never a good idea. By allowing someone to do as they choose without also creating a sufficient level of communication, you are effectively putting yourself "out of the loop" and making yourself vulnerable. In most cases, there is enough trust in the relationship that being a silent partner is not a problem. But in many cases in which someone is unfaithful, it is because there was never sufficient communication in the first place.

- **(FINANCIAL SEX COMPARISON #8) COMMUNICATION IS THE KEY TO MAKING THE EXPERIENCE A GOOD ONE**

The key to good sex, physical or financial is communication. If an individual cannot communicate his/her needs, desires, expectations and problems, then the process can be confusing and disappointing for both parties. What is saddest is that many times, the destruction that comes out of this confusion may have been easily avoided had both parties shared their concerns.

Communication with your partner is critical, and it's something that must occur very early in the process of making financial love. Not only must it occur early in the process, it must occur throughout the process, as needs and issues change through time. Communication not only enhances your ability to work together to reach financial goals, it also ensures that both parties are playing their role in the process.

You can think of communication as a lubricant, like oil. Without proper lubrication, things don't work well together, whether they are engine parts, body parts or social interactions. Many relationships are destroyed due to a lack of communication, in which one partner does not know the needs and expectations of the other.

In my chapters on Financial Foreplay and Oral Sex, we discuss the importance of communication. By communicating and sharing, you can find ways to heighten the pleasure you receive from interacting with your partner.

- **(FINANCIAL SEX COMPARISON #9) IF DONE WELL, YOU CAN REACH HEIGHTS YOU NEVER THOUGHT POSSIBLE**

Any kind of lovemaking process should make you feel better than you felt before you chose to engage in the activity. If you don't feel better about life after you've done the deed, then why waste your time? If a person makes good financial love with you, you both walk away fulfilled, satisfied and blissful. Financial Lovemaking is a process that most, if not all, human beings were built for, since it feeds into our desire to travel the journey of life in pairs, rather than as individuals. I am a believer that life is a journey of love, and Financial Lovemaking is part of that process. It may sound corny to describe life in this way, but think about it: when you are on your death bed, you are not going to think about your job. Such things will seem silly and irrelevant. You are not going to think about your possessions, since you can't take them with you. You are going to think about your family, your personal life, and the love that you experienced along the way. Therefore, I reiterate that life is a journey of love, not much else.

Married couples do much better financially than those that are not married. In fact, 92% of all self-made millionaires are married couples[4]. Some argue that this is due to a number of factors. First, there may be a greater focus on wealth building, since it becomes a more crucial component of each individual's lifestyle. While wealth building may be secondary for the single person, individuals with a family may feel that it's mandatory. Second, there may be greater specialization in the household (i.e. each person does what they are good at and lets the other partner do something else),

---

[4] The Millionaire Mind, Thomas Stanley

where one party stays home while the other focuses on career advancement. This may lead to faster raises and promotions for one party and a reduction in child care expenses for the entire family. Another reason that marriage may build wealth is that there are economies of scale from sharing resources. Economies of scale result from the added benefits of merging your assets. Rather than buying two separate homes, you share a house. Rather than having individual automobiles, a couple may choose to have one car for the entire family. This leads to cost reductions, which can increase the net worth of both individuals.

Generally, if the Financial Lovemaking process is done well, it's both amazing and fulfilling. The hard work necessary to make financial love throughout a lifetime may show itself in greater financial rewards for all parties involved. The key thing to remember is that it must be done TOGETHER, and both parties must be on the same page. If you are disjointed emotionally from your partner, then you will not only find that there are mistakes, deceit and misunderstandings. You will find that the financial and emotional suffering will be both permanent and painful. Working together helps you to avoid many of the problems couples incur when they are not honest about money.

GETTING THE RIGHT BODY FOR FINANCIAL SEX

The average husband says the couple earns 5 percent more income and has 10 percent more total wealth than the wife thinks they have. The average wife says the family's debts are $500 more than reported by her husband. Both husbands and wives report that their spouses earn less than their spouses say they do[5].

[5] Jay Zagorsky, May 2003 *The Journal of Socio-Economics*

There is no point in judging someone else's financial position if you are not in a good one yourself. Financial Lovemaking involves the merging of two financial bodies, and if your body is not at its peak, then your mate may naturally question their desire to merge with you. Similar to when you are considering a physical merger, you might find that a trip to the gym is in order. In addition to trips to the gym, you might also want to take a peek at your eating habits, or in other words, what you are putting into your financial body.

Some people want to merge their finances with someone else so that they can erase the mistakes and flaws in their own lives. On one hand, this makes sense, since relationships should be complementary. On the other hand, it can also be interpreted as being parasitic. First, there could be the guilt of ruining someone else's credit because you have not taken care of your own, or perhaps causing someone else to have to deal with the horrifically high debt that you have created. You may find that they are resentful of the fact that their income is high and yours is low. They are paying for everything and angry that you can't make a serious contribution. Just like a physical relationship, the demons of your past can come back to haunt you. Some mistakes might be forgiven, but in many cases, you are likely to find that your partner resents the fact that you have caused him/her to lose the benefit of years of hard work. Imagine being a neurosurgeon who invested 10 or 15 years of education, only to marry someone who chose not to make the same level of investment? How are you both going to feel when you try to buy your first home, and the bank denies you the loan? How is your partner going to look at you when they feel that you are spending them out of house and home, even though they are earning more than half of the family income? If you are selfish, then you don't care. But if you truly love your partner, you might want to consider working through some of your own issues.

I recommend not considering having financial sex until you are ready. Getting ready doesn't necessarily mean increasing your income, since income isn't everything. It means spending some time working on your own financial habits before getting someone else involved. As you work to change who you are, the last thing you want to hear is someone in your ear about the mistakes you've made, and everything you're doing wrong. At least that's not something I would personally want to hear. It doesn't mean that you can't get married, it just means that you might want to consider taking some time to work on YOU before working on WE. If each of YOU is in good shape, then WE are going to be just fine.

Another thing about having sex without going to the gym is that your partner does not get to see you at your best. Have you ever had that feeling? Think about it. We all go through periods where our bodies are in good shape, and some periods where it's a little bit flabby. Perhaps we put some pounds on during Christmas or we have haven't exercised as much as we should. Would you rather have someone evaluate you during your low points, or during your high points? Well, getting to a high point might mean not allowing someone to see you financially naked until you are good and ready.

I have included a list of some of the things that you might want to think about before deciding to mix your finances with another person. The list is not exhaustive, but it certainly is a good start. These are questions about your "financial body" that you might want to ask to determine whether or not you are ready to have good financial sex with your partner.

FINANCIAL BODY QUESTION #1: ARE YOUR SAVINGS HABITS AS BAD AS THE REST OF AMERICA?

Americans DO NOT SAVE THEIR MONEY. In 2006, the US savings rate was actually *negative*. What does this mean? It means that Americans were borrowing more than they were saving. The only thing that protected them from financial hardship was the fact that their home values were appreciating so quickly. In a USA Today and New York Times story, I stated that "Americans are broke for the same reasons we are fat. We don't choose to have the discipline". This was not meant to make fun of obese Americans. I was making the point that we simply choose to not have the discipline to save. Well, why should we? We are the richest country in the world. Our per capita Gross National Product and average incomes are off the charts, and Americans are spending all of our free time watching shows like "The fabulous life", in which we get to see what kind of diamonds Paris Hilton has put on her dog this week. It's nice when the rest of the world is worried about war and famine, but we get to worry about dog jewelry.

I am not making judgments about the spending habits of Americans. Ok, maybe I am. But they are not harsh judgments. My mother always told me that you can pretty much do whatever you want, as long as you are prepared to endure the consequences of your choices. The consequence of poor savings habits is that you are really putting yourself and your family at risk of financial devastation. If something goes wrong with your job, or your car breaks down, you are basically up a creek without a paddle. This is NOT rocket science. Saving money is not about expertise. It's about having the common sense to simply keep more money in your pocket than you spend every month. Here are some quick tips on how to start a savings program.

1) **Create a budget and pay yourself first.** If you do not know where your money is going, then it is hard to figure out where it went. Keep a budget if you are not already doing so. If you are not sure how to create a budget, my website www.myfinanceprofessor.com shows you how to do it, step by step. When you make your monthly or weekly budget, take out your savings *before* you take out anything for bills or personal spending. Your financial health is more important than anyone else's, and if you don't put yourself first on your personal payroll, then who will?

2) **Put the money in a place that makes it difficult for you to get to it.** I suggest using a mutual fund or bank CD. Don't give yourself an ATM card that basically allows you to get the money back right away.

3) **Set savings goals for yourself, and write them down every other day if you have to.** Remind yourself that you are striving for something that is going to be good for your personal, financial and emotional well-being. You are doing this for yourself, your mate, and your future family. It's worth building your financial future. Setting goals will help you stay focused and motivated as you proceed on your financial journey.

4) **Be consistent.** Put your savings on autopilot, and even consider having the money taken directly out of your paycheck. It will probably make it much easier to see the money grow if you have forgotten about it. Don't check on the balance every week, just pretend that it's another line item being taken out of your paycheck by the federal government.

5) **Consider unconventional ways to save.** When I had a problem saving as a kid, I used to give my money to my grandmother so she could hold it for me. That was a good move for me, because my grandmother was the kind of person who would slice your hands off over a nickel. She would hold the money for 6 months to 1 year, and then I would get it back in a nice, large lump sum.

   Another unconventional way to save money (I think Suzie Orman might kill me for saying this, but it doesn't matter, since I have a PhD and she doesn't – just kidding, I respect Suzie a lot) is to consider adding a few extra dollars to your IRS withholding. The IRS withholding is a line item you fill out on your W-9 form with your employer. They ask you if you would like extra money taken out of your paycheck to be saved for your taxes. Some people might consider this an interest-free loan to the government, but getting your money back without the interest is better than spending your money and not having anything to show for it. The steps in learning to save are baby ones, so you can't expect yourself to be perfect right off the bat. Anything that moves you closer to spending less than you earn is a good thing.

FINANCIAL BODY QUESTION #2: DO YOU HAVE MORE DEBT THAN THE FEDERAL GOVERNMENT?

Unlike Dave Ramsey and some of the other so-called "Financial gurus", I am not anti-debt. For some reason, there are a ton of financial advisors who tell you to avoid debt at all costs. They are WRONG. Well, most of the time they are wrong. They joke that there is no such thing as "good debt" vs. "bad debt". Well, the reality is that they simply may not fully understand the nature of debt.

Many of the greatest companies in America were founded using debt. When debt is widely available to American businesses, our economy prospers. During the Savings and Loan Crisis in the early 90s, the lack of available debt led to a major economic downturn. *Debt is good for our economy, and it can also be good for your life.*

I know that my position on debt is a radical concept for most. However, you should think of debt like a really fast car: It can help you achieve some things, but it can also get you into trouble if you are not responsible. The responsible use of debt for a productive purpose is not usually a bad thing. The same can be said for drugs, fire or any other powerful thing in our society.

When debt is a good thing

Here is an example of a case in which debt is a really good thing. Let's say that you earn $20,000 per year as a waitress and you chose not to go to college (some waitresses have gone to college, so no offense to those who did). But you know that if you go to college, your income will increase to

$50,000 per year with a degree in business. Not only are you going to earn more money, but your long-term salary growth rate is going to be higher, you are going to have greater job satisfaction (hopefully, if you choose a career you enjoy) and you are likely to have much more job security than you would without any education.

So, lets say that in order to pay for college for 4 years, you are forced to borrow $10,000 per year for tuition (you are not going to choose the most expensive school, nor the cheapest), plus another $10,000 per year for living expenses. That gives you a total of $80,000 in debt once you have completed 4 years of college.

Let's get to the math. This is not a precise calculation by any stretch, since precise analysis would require adjustments for inflation, interest earned on money, as well as raises and bonuses (my website, www.myfinanceprofessor.com provides more details if you would like to see them). But the calculation here is a relatively conservative one, and gets to the point I am trying to make:

Extra salary earned over the next 30 years (not including raises and bonuses): 30 x $30,000 = $900,000
Total loan repayment ($80,000 in loans, plus roughly $50,000 in interest) = $130,000

Profit = Salary – loan = $900,000 - $130,000 = $770,000.

The point being made in this simple calculation is not a complicated one. *Borrowing money is only bad when you are not going to earn more than you borrow.* In the case of education, buying a home or starting a business, debt can be a very good thing. In fact, I would not want to live in a world without debt.

When debt is a bad thing

With all this being said above, I should discuss the other side of debt. The scary side of debt is that it creates something called "leverage". Leverage is defined, basically, as placing yourself in a risky situation that could hurt you financially if things go wrong. If you are "highly levered", it means that you will either be way up or way down, like a really long see-saw. Part of The Great Depression was blamed on our country's excessive use of debt to finance stock market purchases. When the market was going well, things were happy and good. Children were laughing and playing, and people felt richer than a fat man in a bowl of ice cream. When the market crashed, many investors were unable to repay their loans with their existing assets, which led them to have to sell their stocks to raise the cash. When everyone in the stock market is selling at the same time, this creates a downward spiral on stock prices, making the crash even worse.

The same thing can happen in your own life. If you have high debt, you are exposing yourself to a great deal of risk. Companies that loan you money expect a fixed loan payment, and they do not care what is going on with your personal financial life. If you lose your job, or your wealth suddenly drops, you are still forced to deal with the debt. This doesn't even count the extraordinarily high interest charges that you may be forced to pay.

For these reasons, you should get rid of as much of your bad debt as you possibly can. After you get rid of your bad debt, you should then focus on your good debt. The **wrong** reasons to borrow money might include the following list below:

1) **Buying a new car**

Cars depreciate as soon as you drive them off the lot. I am not one to condemn certain types of borrowing, but I have a hard time figuring out why people would want to borrow large amounts of money for a new car. If you want a nice car, you should probably just save half the down payment in cash, and then get a car that is a year or two old. New cars tend to be the worst bargains in the world.

Another thing that makes auto debt the worst kind to have is that you can usually identify bad debt by how long the asset lasts. If you are still making payments after the asset has lost its value, chances are you should not have taken that particular loan. After about 3 – 4 years, you are usually making payments on a financial ghost haunting you from your past indiscretions, since the car's value has usually eroded a great deal by year 3.

2) **Borrowing to buy new clothes, jewelry, electronics and other counter-productive extras**

This is what gets most Americans into trouble. That little bit of debt just piles and piles, and before long, you've got a ton of credit card debt. I recommend buying the "counter-productive extras" with cash, and then stopping yourself after your cash runs out. Sometimes, you have to avoid the mall as if you are a recovering drug addict staying out of the crackhouse. As I discuss later, knowing how to control your spending is a personal process requiring that you understand the source of your bad habits.

Also, be wary of opening credit card accounts that allow you to shop at a specific store. Usually, discounts are associated with filling out the application, which are designed to trick you into spending more money. These cards are usually the worst kinds of credit you can obtain, and they get you into financial trouble very quickly.

3) Nearly any kind of credit card debt

Credit card companies are amazing. They have somehow convinced Americans that their loans are actually free money. They not only hit you with high interest charges in many cases, but they sometimes hit you with fees: the over limit fee, the late fee, the annual fee, and any other kind of fee they can think of. You must understand that these additional fees are underhanded ways for banks to get extra money out of your pocket, and to charge you additional interest. Don't just look at the interest rate on the card as your primary cost, check out the fee structure as well. Most of the time, credit card debt is not good for you, and there are few healthy ways to use credit cards. Finding a healthy way to use a lot of credit cards is almost like trying to find health-conscious ways to smoke cigarettes. Usually, the best way to smoke is to not smoke at all, and the same is true for most credit cards.

4) Borrowing for something you don't need

Distinguishing between wants and needs is critical if you want to manage your debt. I recommend only borrowing for needs that are immediate. In fact, if you really think about it, many of the things that we think we need are actually things that we want. Making this distinction is critical, since it has a powerful impact on your ability to manage wealth.

5) Borrowing money for another person who might not pay it back.

I am not sure why anyone in their right mind would borrow money for another person, especially a friend. This magnifies the problems created by debt because not only are you worried about your own financial situation, you are worried about someone's else's, which you cannot control. Unless there is a very good reason for doing so, borrowing money for someone else is an absolute no-no. This holds especially true if you are borrowing for someone you love. Leverage is one thing, but you do not want to put leverage on your personal relationship, which can be easily destroyed by money.

Sandy and Dave loved one another very much, but were not quite ready for marriage. In spite of the fact that Dave wanted to marry Sandy, she had other plans and felt that marriage would cramp her ability to enjoy her life and career. Dave, in his willingness to do anything for Sandy, co-signed on a car loan for a new Ford Taurus that she could not quite get enough credit to purchase. Rather than wondering why no one else in the world was willing to help Sandy buy a car, Dave simply felt that it was because she was misunderstood, and no one knew how responsible she really could be. Other than a few slips and mishaps, he'd felt that she was always a model financial citizen. Or so he thought, based on what he knew about her financial habits.

What Dave didn't know was that Sandy's creditors had good reason for not lending her money. She had over $30,000 in credit card debt, paid most of her bills late (or when she felt like it), and had creditors calling her for money every two days. He didn't realize that rather than dealing with creditors, Sandy simply hung up on them and pretended that they didn't exist. She did the same thing to the auto financer *when they called asking for payments on the car. If all of her money had been spent at the mall, she would simply conclude that she could make the payments the following month.*

This ruined Dave's credit, as he became the next person in line for companies to go after in the event that Sandy did not pay up. He became frustrated, as she would get angry at him if he brought up her poor payment habits, and she considered his persistent hounding to be a sign of disrespect. Eventually, Dave found Sandy sleeping with another man in his bed, after which she confessed that she didn't love him anymore. Part of her reason for leaving him was that he'd become a "controlling, hyper-sensitive wet blanket" with all of his nagging about money. Sandy eventually started a relationship with another man, and years later, Dave's name is still on the cosign agreement for the car that Sandy is driving today.

6) Borrowing for purchases that have no value after the purchase is made

"Consumption-based purchases" is my term for purchases that involve things that are not going to have much value after the purchase is made. This sort of borrowing (i.e. using credit cards, bank loans or any other kind of loan) usually includes borrowing for vacations, meals, entertainment or other things that have no value at all. Remember what I said before about making payments on a ghost? Well, these products basically become ghosts the minute the purchase has been made! There is NOTHING worse than making long-term payments on things that you don't even remember buying in the first place. This is the worst kind of debt there is.

REDUCING YOUR DEBT IN PREPARATION FOR FINANCIAL LOVEMAKING

If you want to get ready for the lovemaking process, find a way to reduce your debt. Attack the small debt first, the credit cards, and other small loans that you can kill very easily. Then, try to find ways to consolidate the larger debts, such as student loans, and other things you owe. This will communicate to your partner that you acknowledge your high debt levels, but you are being responsible in terms of working to get them reduced. This will lead him/her to respect you for your diligence and personal responsibility in the Financial Lovemaking process.

If you use the computer program Microsoft Excel and are comfortable with it, create a spreadsheet that shows where your debt level will go over the next 2 – 3 years if you are paying it down consistently. If you are not comfortable with this program, then simply write out a plan on paper (I give an example below). This will give you something to strive for and serves as a reminder that you are on the right path. There is a saying that says: No matter what you are today, you are always BECOMING something tomorrow. It's not a matter what you are now. What matters is what you are becoming in the long-run. By managing your debt responsibly, you are becoming a more financially competent and confident person. And who doesn't enjoy merging assets with someone who is financially capable? The same way it is fun to merge with a person who is sexually capable, a satisfying financial merger can be rewarding as well.

Sample debt reduction plan

My goal: to eliminate $5,000 in credit card debt

How I am going to do this: By stopping the use of credit cards for anything other than emergencies, by paying $250 per month and by cutting expenses in other areas of my budget in order to make my plan more affordable.

The Spreadsheet is below:

Month	Beg of month	Interest	Payment	End of month
1	5,000	75	250	4,825
2	4,825	72.375	250	4,647
3	4,647	69.71063	250	4,467
4	4,467	67.00628	250	4,284
5	4,284	64.26138	250	4,098
6	4,098	61.4753	250	3,910
7	3,910	58.64743	250	3,718
8	3,718	55.77714	250	3,524
9	3,524	52.8638	250	3,327
10	3,327	49.90675	250	3,127
11	3,127	46.90536	250	2,924
12	2,924	43.85894	250	2,718
13	2,718	40.76682	250	2,509
14	2,509	37.62832	250	2,296
15	2,296	34.44275	250	2,081
16	2,081	31.20939	250	1,862
17	1,862	27.92753	250	1,640
18	1,640	24.59644	250	1,414
19	1,414	21.21539	250	1,186
20	1,186	17.78362	250	953
21	953	14.30037	250	718
22	718	10.76488	250	478
23	478	7.176353	250	236
24	236	3.533998	250	-11

Notice that in the above spreadsheet, it is going to take 24 months to get rid of this debt, if you assume that the interest rate is 18% per year (you don't see 18%, but that's the number used to create the spreadsheet. If you are not comfortable creating a spreadsheet like this on your own, and you want to figure out how long it would take you to eliminate a certain amount of debt, here is a rule of thumb you can use:

- Divide the annual interest rate on the credit card by 12. This is approximately how much you pay in interest every month.

- Next, multiply your total balance by this number (so, if your annual rate is 18%, divide that by 12 to get 1.5%. Multiplying 1.5% times a balance of $5,000 gives you $75 in monthly interest).

- Multiply the monthly interest number by 3.5. In this case, 3.5 * 75 = $262.5. This is your monthly payment if you want to pay the debt off in less than 2 years.

I recommend not attacking all the debt you have at once. This could be overwhelming. I recommend breaking it into $5,000 chunks and attacking one block at a time. If you have other debt, you can make minimum payments to keep the balance in tact, and then go after that debt later. Remember: it's easier to eat an elephant one bite at a time. Don't let the debt reduction process overwhelm you.

FINANCIAL BODY QUESTION #3: DO YOU SPEND LIKE YOU HAVE NO COMMON CENTS?

When I teach personal finance, I love to use a particular term with my students. The term is "spendaholic". I use this term because I see overspending to be similar to any other kind of hyper-indulgence: overeating, using drugs, or drinking alcohol. All of these things can be done in moderation, but there are some who do them incessantly. Americans have a horrible problem when it comes to overspending, mainly because our culture is driven by consumption, credit cards, and many other things that can put us into financial jeopardy.

A spendaholic is similar to an alcoholic. Answer this questionnaire to determine if you might be a spendaholic. These questions are not meant to embarrass or chastise you. They are simply meant to encourage you to study your own spending habits to see if they can be improved:

1. If you have money in your pocket, do you tend to spend till every penny is gone? (oversatiation)

2. Do you like to shop or spend because you are bored or feeling emotionally down? (emotional spending)

3. Do you find yourself broke before every paycheck, and not sure where all the money went (money binging)

4. Do you ever go shopping (and eventually spend money) without having anything in mind that you want to purchase? (compulsive spending)

5. If you lost your job today, would you be able to survive on your savings for more than 2 months? If you were to significantly reduce your spending today, would this be any different? (careless spending)

6. Do you use credit cards for things other than big ticket items? If so, do you take longer than 1 month to repay the balance? (petty spending)

7. If you run out of cash in the mall, what do you do: a) go right to the ATM, b) find another source of payment or c) stop shopping and go home? (negative self-enablement)

8. Do you find that you frequently feel worse after you've spent a lot of money and have nothing left, as if you've done something wrong? (Spender's guilt)

9. If you could go back in time for one year, would you change the amount of money you spent? (Regretful spending)

10. Are you quick to buy things for other people, such as meals, clothing, etc.? (Life of the Party Spending)

If you answered yes to more than 2 or 3 of these questions, you might be a spendaholic. I'm not Dr. Phil, and I am not going to try to be an arm chair psychologist. But as a researcher in Financial Psychology, these are warning signs that a person has a tendency to overspend.

I am not saying that you shouldn't spend. Spending is fun, and money is meant to be enjoyed in addition to being put to productive uses. The point is that most spendaholics spend beyond the point of satiation (the point of satiation is when you are satisfied and have all you need). Spendaholics do not spend because they need something, they spend because they need to spend. The same can be said for overeating, when a person eats beyond the point of being hungry. Now, if you sometimes engage in meaningless spending, it doesn't mean that you are a spendaholic. It is only a concern if your spending continues to put you into situations that make you unhappy. Usually, the cues for overeating are not related to hunger; it might be watching TV, being sad or depressed, feeling bored, or just knowing that the food is there. Overspending is similar in that we may shop because we are in a store, because we have nothing else to do, or the money is "burning a hole in our pocket". An additional symptom of overspending is that your regret what you've done after you've finished. In addition to regret, your bad habits continue to put you into risky and challenging situations. There is no one way to define overspending, but all of these symptoms may apply.

Being a spendaholic can be highly destructive to the financial love-making process. It can destroy everything you work for, and it will lead to more arguments with your mate than you care to know. Therefore, it's *critical* to get your spending habits under control before engaging in Financial Lovemaking. Engaging in Financial Lovemaking as a spendaholic is similar to making love as a sex addict: Your selfish actions are going to always allow external factors to destroy the one-on-one relationship you have with your partner. Here are some tips for the recovering spendaholic:

1) Consider becoming an "investaholic":

While going from overspending to saving is admirable, it's incredibly difficult. The next best thing to not spending is to at least spend your money on things that are going to add financial value to your life. A spendaholic doesn't always care what he/she is spending their money on. All some care about is that they are spending. The same might be true for an overweight person. Sometimes, they will simply eat what is in the fridge, whether it is carrots or candy bars. Why not stuff the fridge with healthy food and let him/her eat away?

So, consider starting a business or investment plan that you can put your money into. Start the business in something that you really enjoy, so that it's pleasurable to you, rather than a burden. Then, if you have the urge to overspend, put the money into your business. This is similar to someone who overeats, but instead of eating chips and cookies all the time, they overeat with vegetables and fruit. Sure, not eating at all would be good, but eating healthy is the next best thing.

Of course, your long term objective is to eventually learn to save. You don't want to catch yourself putting all of your cash into an investment, only to find that you end up bankrupt due to a lack of liquid reserves (liquid reserves basically means cash available to you to pay bills. You can sometimes have a lot of wealth without having cash – for example, you may have real estate or valuable art that would be difficult to sell in a financial bind).

2) Remember: Not everything that's fun costs money

One problem with spendaholics is that they may feel that spending money is the only way to have a good time. I have gone to a few night clubs where they sell bottles of alcohol for over $200 each, or incredibly expensive restaurants where the food doesn't taste much better than fast food. I am not saying that you shouldn't ever spend money, but if you take a look before spending money on things that may or may not be worth the price, you might find that you can do without the thing that you are about to give up next month's rent in order to purchase.

There are numerous resources in the world that don't cost a dime, and it would help you to explore those resources more diligently. Why not spend time in the park with your mate, rather than going to a mall? Why not rent a movie or see what's on cable, instead of going to a movie theatre? Having friends over can be better than going out with them. Why not have a picnic in your living room instead of going out to expensive night clubs? Why not purchase ready made pizza crust and your own toppings, instead of purchasing a pizza from a shop? There are a lot of ways to have fun, and you don't have to spend money to enjoy them.

3) **Keep the money out of your hands!**

The only way that money can "burn a hole in your pocket" is if the money is in your pocket in the first place. A recovering spendaholic with too much cash is no different from an alcoholic who keeps a bottle of vodka in the back seat. Keep money out of your pockets, and do not allow yourself to use credit cards. But don't be cruel to yourself. Set a spending limit in advance by giving yourself a set cash allowance, and force yourself to limit your spending to some amount below the given level of the allowance. Make the allowance amount generous, as long as you can afford it. Then, when you go out, only take one credit card, and don't allow yourself to use it for anything other than emergencies. If you can't afford to pay cash for something, then the rule is that you can't afford to buy it.

4) **Make some notes**

One day, when you're bored, sit and write down exactly how much money you earn every month. After that, write down all of your bills, including rent, utilities, car notes, internet connections, the cable bill, child support, charitable contributions, getting your hair done, and any other bill you have. Next, subtract the amount you pay in bills from the amount you earn and study the difference. *This is how much money you waste every month if you are not saving.*

Then, take the total of all income minus bills and divide it by 4. This is approximately how much money you waste every week. Try to reconcile the money wasted every week with what you spend money on. Think about shopping trips, outings, and other incidentals you incur during a typical week. Most of us cannot reconcile the two. That's because one of the first problems that a spendaholic has is that he does not know where his money is going. This is similar to an overweight person who has no idea how many calories they take in during a given day. I am not calling you a spendaholic, you may not be one. However, most Americans have some of the tendencies of spendaholics, particularly in the age of easy credit cards.

Start by again writing down how much you earn every month. Then, you want to carefully control where this money is going. You don't have to keep receipts and detailed notes on every transaction (unless you want to). You can actually just create constraints that will allow you to know where your money is going. For example, lets say that Missy earns $3,000 per month after taxes and other things are taken out of her paycheck. Assume that her household bills are $1500. That means that, theoretically, she has $1500 that can be used for saving and investing. But given that she is a spendaholic, she finds that the $1500 goes right down the drain. When she divides this number by 4, she finds that she has $375 each week that she is spending on items that are above and beyond her monthly bills.

She then deducts the cost of lunch every day ($30 per week), gas ($30), and going out to dinner and a movie on the weekend ($40). This totals $100 per week, and she has no idea where the other $275 has gone. What she has not counted are the interest charges she pays on her credit cards after going on random shopping sprees that have piled up over the years ($30 per week). She also doesn't count on the fact that she and her best friend always find a "once in a lifetime special" at the mall each Saturday ($120 per week). Additionally, she doesn't count the fact that she usually goes to Starbucks every single day for a café latte and chocolate muffin ($30 per week). These expenses, along with other little ones, have slowly, but surely eaten away at her finances, to the point that she doesn't realize that her financial body is becoming bloated with unnecessary costs. This is no different from smoking cigarettes and drinking beer every day and then years later, wondering why you have a big belly, black lungs and yellow teeth.

What might be her solution?

Missy could start by simply making careful note of how much she has available for spending. Taking notes helps Missy develop a concrete idea about how much money she is realistically able to spend each month. She has already done this, which is the first step toward confronting her poor spending and saving habits.

Secondly, ***Missy can set parameters for herself.*** If her goal is to save $500 per month out of the extra $1500 she has in disposable income, then she should give herself only $250 per week for spending cash. This is an ample amount of money for Missy to spend, giving her plenty of room for error. It's similar to an overweight person giving himself a very large plate of food on the condition that this is the only plate he can eat (I do this to myself when I want to lose weight). Setting parameters, even small ones, can make a huge difference in our lives. Sometimes, it's all about having limits.

Missy then has to make sure there is no "leakage" in her saving, spending and investing plan. What do I mean by leakage? I am referring to spending that occurs outside of that which is expected in the family budget. Leakage can happen when we do not plan for all necessary costs in our lives and end up deviating from our savings plan. She should automate her monthly bills so that the only bills being paid are the ones on the budget. If she forgets something, she needs to adjust the monthly budget. If there is an unexpected expense, she should try to either delay it, or take it out of her cash allowance.

Finally, Missy should keep her credit cards at home. The rule for spending should be this: Spend all you want, but don't spend more than you have in your cash account. That means that she should cap her spending to what she allows herself in cash. This is how she can keep track of where her money is going. She may not keep track of every little detail of her spending, but I am not a fan of anal record keeping anyway. As long as she has good estimates of where the money is going, this works out just fine. Remember: money is meant to be enjoyed, and so is life. The key is to do things in moderation.

FINANCIAL BODY QUESTION #4: IS YOUR CREDIT SCORE LOWER THAN A DWARF ON HIS KNEES? (NO OFFENSE TO LITTLE PEOPLE, OF COURSE)

Credit scores are a funny thing. They follow us around and stress us out to no end. Also, any little problem on your credit report can cause you to spend days on the phone correcting the error. This is not a fun part of managing your money. But as you might already know, your credit score makes the difference between getting that house you always wanted vs. paying rent to a landlord until you die.

The conventional wisdom about credit reports is that there are "5 C's of good credit". They are generally represented as the following:

1) Character
2) Capacity
3) Collateral
4) Capital
5) Condition

"Character" relates to whether or not you show a history of paying your bills on time. If you don't pay things on time, or you stiff your creditors on a regular basis, then they decide that you are officially a "bad person". Perhaps they might also assume that you are a lazy or irresponsible person, I am not sure.

"Capacity" reflects your ability to repay what you owe. So, if you have a job earning $10,000 per year, you probably don't have the capacity to get that $100,000 loan. This stuff is measured by looking at things like your financial liquidity, which measures how much you have in savings and assets that are easily converted to cash. It's also measured by your annual income.

"Collateral" is the stuff you own which protects your lender from the fact that you might decide not to pay the loan back (otherwise known as "default"). Collateral could be your home, your car, or perhaps your dog, if you have one of the fluffy ones that smell like sexy perfume (just kidding). Either way, you are going to usually have to secure your loans with something, especially when you are attempting to borrow a lot of money. By "secure", I am referring to something that the bank gets to keep in the event that you do not repay.

"Capital" basically refers to how much "stuff" you own in general. This differs from collateral in that collateralized assets are specifically promised to the lender in the event that you can't repay. Capital just means that you own a lot of things, some of which is not collateralized. So, as you can guess, rich folks have a lot of capital.

"Condition" reflects how your income might change if economic conditions change. So, if the country goes into a recession, are you likely to lose your job? Well, if you have a 5-year contract, then the likelihood is much lower than if you are, say, a seasonal worker. This simply reflects risk, and the bottom line is that no one wants to loan you anything if you are a risky investment. An example of a risky profession might be owning your own business or doing seasonal work.

The 5 C's of credit all impact your credit score in various ways. There are several formulas that show the weight of each variable, but honestly, no one knows the true formula. The key is to be mindful of these factors when you manage your credit, so that you can maximize your own score. Also, you should check your credit score every 3 months, look for errors and dispute any problems that you find.

SPECIAL CREDIT PROBLEMS THAT WOMEN CAN HAVE

At the risk of sounding sexist, I want to briefly discuss special credit issues that relate to women. If you are not married and don't plan on doing so, then this section may not be for you. But if you are thinking about tying the knot, you may want to consider how marriage can affect your credit.

Getting married and having a name change can make your financial situation more complicated, as the credit bureaus may only know you as Mrs. ________. Additionally, there is the problem of using inconsistent titles. For example, one minute, a woman may call herself "Mrs. Jane Wilson", and the next minute she may use "Mrs. John Wilson". This leads to inconsistencies when trying to create a credit history.

One way to get around this problem is to ensure that you use the same name on all credit applications. Also, it's important that when you apply for credit, you use both your name and your husband's name, and not simply allow your husband to handle all credit situations. A final point is to ensure that you have your own credit file, and not just one that is shared with your mate.

Another problem that women have had in the past when it comes to credit is the fact that their careers can be interrupted due to child bearing plans. This career interruption can lead to discrimination by potential creditors, who may consider bearing children to be a sign that you may have an inconsistent ability to repay your debts. The Equal Credit Opportunity Act is designed to alleviate this form of discrimination, and it makes it illegal for a potential creditor to check into a woman's marital status or child-bearing plans when considering her for credit.

Obviously, divorce can cause credit problems for both women and men, as you can end up paying for the purchases of someone who doesn't even love you anymore. This is one of the reasons that credit management is such an important part of the Financial Lovemaking process.

MANAGING YOUR CREDIT – STEPS YOU CAN TAKE

Whether you have stellar credit, or credit so bad that they won't even take your cash, there are steps you can take to at least show your lover that you care about your credit and about your joint financial future. It can take a while to fix a credit problem, but if you put the corrective measures on autopilot and take care of them one at a time, you will soon find yourself on the path toward financial bliss.

1) **Get a copy of your credit report every other month**

There are three credit reporting agencies that you can use: Experian, Transunion and Equifax. You can get a report from any of these three agencies, but I recommend that you get a report from all three of them. A site such as www.myfico.com can help you find your credit reports, as well as sell you a ton of other junk that you might want to purchase. I don't buy the extra stuff, I just get my credit report and keep rolling.

After you get the reports, you should notice that first off, they are not all the same. Different agencies record different information, and I am not sure how each agency decides what is important and what's not. Second, you should go through each line of the report and make sure you recognize everything on the report. Take a look at things that have been recorded recently, and take a peek at things that have been on your report for a while. Given that this is an important part of your financial life, you should probably invest the time to familiarize yourself with your credit report and how to read it.

2) **Sign up for automatic alerts on your credit**

When you go to FICO or any other place, you will have the chance to sign up for some of their other services. I enjoy receiving automatic updates via email. Here, they can tell you if someone changes something on your credit report, or if someone has presented good or bad information about you. This allows you to keep up with things as they change. It also alerts you if people have been checking your credit report regularly. It's a great tool to avoid identity theft as well, since you are constantly connected to changes in your credit status.

3) Fix the things that are hurting your credit

Don't assume that because something is on your credit report, it's automatically correct. Credit bureaus make mistakes all the time, and many times, companies report inaccurate information about you. You can sometimes have things removed from your credit report by simply disputing them in a letter. In the letter, you can at least have the company verify that the debt is yours, or that you didn't make the payments when you were asked to do so. That way, you can find out what documentation exists to verify the debt that you owe. An amendment to the Fair Credit Reporting Act requires that creditors respond to your letters of inquiry within 30 days, or they must remove the negative information from your credit report.

There was a time when it was a complete mystery as to what was used to create a credit score. Now, rather than the process being a complete mystery, it's just a substantial mystery. But the box has been opened recently in terms of sharing credit score components with consumers. In general, The Fair Isaac Corporation (FICO) has defined the five factors that go into a credit score. They are

1. Payment history (roughly 35% of the score)
2. Outstanding debt (30%)
3. Credit history (15%)
4. The number of new credit inquiries (10%)
5. Other (10%)

While this formula is not precise, it gives you some idea of what factors matter most in determining your credit score.

4) Consider using a credit counselor to make everything right

Credit counselors are people that work with individuals and families to help them rectify their money problems. This might involve helping to establish a budget, or working as an intermediary between the individual and his/her creditors. Either way, a good financial counselor can be as important as a good couples counselor.

The Consumer Credit Counseling Service is one good place to go if you want help. They are a nonprofit, reputable organization, so your chances of getting "hoodwinked" are lower than they would be otherwise. I still recommend doing your own homework however, to ensure that the organization is reputable. I also recommend making sure that you do not sign on with a repayment plan you cannot afford.

When it comes to credit counselors, they are not all created equal. Some of them do a very good job for you, while others do a good job of taking your money. There are companies set up to exploit desperate consumers by making empty promises about being able to instantly fix your credit. Most of these companies are not able to deliver on any aspect of that promise. However, there are ways to find a credit counselor that fits your needs. We'll discuss these tactics later in the book when credit repair is analyzed in greater detail.

The key to getting your credit and financial situation together is commitment. If you are determined to improve your credit, and you stick with it, then your score will rise. You owe this to yourself, and you owe it to your partner.

FINANCIAL BODY QUESTION #5: DOES YOUR ANNUAL INCOME MAKE A WELFARE CHECK LOOK GOOD?

Let's be honest, not all of us earn the amount of money we once thought we would. Some of us never thought money was important in the first place. Some of us didn't realize how important it would become to us as we got older. There's no "shame in your game", since most of us make mistakes in our lives. But regardless of how you got there, you may find yourself broke as a joke, and the joke isn't even funny. What's worse is that you might question your ability to bring something to the table in the Financial Lovemaking process. If there were such a thing as Financial Viagra, this would be a great time to use it.

Whether you think it's fair or not, there usually isn't as much pressure on women to bring home the same amount of money as a man. However, there are consequences for women and men if they don't possess a sufficient degree of financial leverage in a relationship. By "financial leverage", I am simply referring to power. Some partners seem to feel that the individual with less money should have less control in a relationship. I'm not a fan of either marital partner deciding to leave the entire earning process to the other partner, since that makes the non-earning partner quite vulnerable. At the very least, you should understand that allowing someone else to "bring home ALL the bacon" may expose you to a set of risks that you have to be sure to minimize and manage. We'll talk more about these risks when we ask the question "Does size really matter?"

One other thing about income that you have to remember: It's not static throughout your life, it's dynamic. That means that it can change through time. But things are not usually going to change if you don't make a serious commitment to improving your situation. Given that you are reading this book, chances are that you are not too old to make constructive changes to your income situation. Let's talk about that now.

STRATEGIES TO INCREASE YOUR INCOME

Obviously, the greatest sources of income for most Americans are their jobs. Some of us are lucky and get money from other sources: Alimony and child support, owning our own businesses, or a huge inheritance. But if you are like most Americans, chances are that you work for a living. I believe there are three sources of potential satisfaction from a job, and they all start with the letter "S". They are: "Security", "Salary" and "Satisfaction". These three words are important as you evaluate your job and its compensation. If you are switching professions and increasing your salary, it wouldn't make sense to give up too much job security or satisfaction. On the other hand, I am a believer that there is almost no amount of money worth having a job that you hate.

The career you choose is not just going to affect your partner financially, it can affect them emotionally as well. For example, if you earn a high salary and have no job security, your partner has to endure the stress of worrying about whether or not you are going to keep your position. Or, if you have great job security, a high salary and no satisfaction, then he/she has to deal with the emotional turmoil created by an unsatisfied mate. All of these factors must be considered as you elevate your status and determine how well your job compensates you.

A person without a very high salary can find a multitude of ways to increase his annual income. Some of these options might be open to you, some may not. But if you are creative and persistent, there's always a path toward improvement.

Additional Education

Ever think about going back to school? This is always an option, no matter how old you are. As you know, there is that commonly cited statistic which estimates that a college graduate earns a million dollars more in their lifetime than a high school graduate. It's never too late to go back and earn a Bachelors or Masters Degree. Additional education may not always lead to a higher salary, but it can very easily lead to other forms of additional compensation. The compensation may come from the fact that your educational credentials create options for you. If you don't like your current position, you can consider moving to another one. You may also have additional job satisfaction created from the fact that you are free to study whatever field you find most interesting. This can lead to a much happier life, and in turn a happier life for your partner.

Some would say that it makes sense to make these major career changes BEFORE getting involved deeply with someone else. Having another person involved in the job selection process can lead to a reduction in the number of options you have, given that you are forced to accommodate the life choices of another person, as well as their needs and interests. You may find that the best nursing jobs are in Minnesota, while your partner has a family and job in Alabama. Having a family situation can often place additional financial pressure upon you.

There is another school of thought which states that going back to school after "getting hooked up" can be easier if your partner is supportive of your decision. If you are earning a low wage, your partner can take up the slack, thus allowing you to pursue your education. The short-coming of such thinking might be the assumption that your significant other is going to remain completely patient and supportive of your choices. We all know that all human beings have needs, and going back to school may have indirectly caused divorce, or in some cases, infidelity.

Personally, I had a very good friend whose parents worked together to put her father through medical school. Everything seemed fine on the surface, but beneath, there were problems brewing: major marital problems ranging from infidelity, loneliness, unmet needs, and growing distrust and resentment. Rather than the family growing closer after graduation, the long hours of a physician and the pressures life in the Emergency Room took additional tolls on the family. Divorce followed soon thereafter.

Starting a business

Most people who work for someone else have never seriously considered working for themselves. If they have thought about it, it's usually just a pipe dream. Personally, I feel that if you can pull it off, self-employment can be one of the most satisfying lives you can possibly live. At the same time, starting a business doesn't mean you have to create a multimillion dollar enterprise. It simply means that you have to create a stream of revenue doing something that you want to do. It might mean providing a service or selling something small to your friends. Either way, it can both increase your income and reduce your tax bill at the end of the year.

I recommend sitting with yourself and thinking about things you would like to do. Then, try to think of an unmet need that you can fill, perhaps cooking for people, or selling a product. If you enjoy doing it, then it won't seem like work at all. This might open the door for additional revenue for you, which will make you a more ideal partner for Financial

Lovemaking. Through time, you will find that your revenue stream continues to grow, and your small side business has become a substantial piece of the family revenue. As an aside, if you get divorced, your mate will have a tough time getting a big chunk of the business you've created, especially if they are not working for you directly.

Working overtime

Can you work overtime or get a part-time job? If you have extra time, you should never consider free time to be O.K. to waste. Time is a precious commodity, one of the most precious you will ever own. If you have extra time, why not spend some of that time either earning more money or figuring out ways to make some?

A little overtime (if available) is also a nice way to create a financial nest egg by saving the additional funds coming into the household. Keep this in mind as you plan to tie the knot one day, while having plenty of financial rope in your pocket.

Getting into a new profession

No matter your age, you are NEVER locked into your given profession. You might feel trapped because that is the only thing that you've done up until this point. But you are NOT trapped, if you free your mind. There are many ways to skin a cat, meaning that you can earn a living doing quite a few things, not just the same things you've done for the past several years. This is especially true if you are under the age of 45. In fact, most 32 year olds without a college degree can still go to medical school if they choose and end up practicing medicine by the time they reach their 40s. You then have another 25 – 30 years to benefit from your hard work. If that is true for switching into medicine, then it's especially true for fields such as Accounting or Engineering.

I once heard a woman contemplate going back to school and switching careers completely. The woman was 36, and she didn't feel that she was young enough to make a major career change. She said "By the time I go to school for 4 years and graduate, I'll be 40 years old." Her career counselor, being a wise and patient individual, simply said to her "Well, you're going to turn 40 anyway. Wouldn't you rather be 40 doing something you love?" This led the woman to change careers, and she hasn't looked back ever since.

Cut costs and expenses (a penny saved....)

It's said "A penny saved is a penny earned". I agree with this statement, because it explains a basic concept: *You can increase your income by simply reducing your expenses.* Most of us have a lot of "fat" in our budgets. Americans, by nature, are "financially chubby". Many of the things we consider to be necessities are really luxury items.

I encourage you to go through your life with a fine-tooth comb and find the fat that you can cut. One way to do this would be to destroy your monthly budget. Then, rebuild it slowly, justifying each line item as you go along. This is something that the federal government does periodically, in order to find the fat in its own budget (well, that might be a bad example, since the government can be incredibly wasteful, but I'm sure you get the point).

THINKING ABOUT THE KIND OF PARTNER WHO IS GOING TO COMPLEMENT YOU FINANCIALLY

It's nice to believe that money and love have nothing to do with one another, but that would be a big, fat lie! I've always wondered why celebrities become hotter and better-looking to women once they sign their latest ten million dollar contract. Now this doesn't necessarily mean that we've become a nation of gold diggers. Maybe it implies that we are simply human beings with real needs. Some of these needs, such as money or sex, might be taboo, but they are very real. I personally feel that the more honest you are with yourself about your needs, the happier you are. If you like tall men and you force yourself to date a short guy, you might end up spending the rest of your life drooling over basketball players.

When it comes to money, the Financial Lovemaking process obviously involves complementarities: finding the mate who can constructively add to the things you bring to the table. For example, if you do not have a very high income, then perhaps it's important to find a partner who has a higher income than you. Or, perhaps your partner can complement you in terms of job security. If you are an aspiring actor with an unsteady income, then an Accountant with a steady job might be the best choice for a mate.

Of course these decisions should never be made in a vacuum. Being with someone only for money is almost always a bad idea. But if their financial situation supplements your own, it can lead to an enhanced quality of life. The life choices *you* make should be taken into consideration as you evaluate the life choices of your partner.

THINKING ABOUT NON-FINANCIAL WAYS YOU CAN CONTRIBUTE TO A RELATIONSHIP

There are clearly many ways one can contribute to the Financial Lovemaking process without bringing in money. Remember: money is valuable, but it's only one of many valuable assets a person can own. Love, commitment, energy, happiness, or even physical intimacy can be valuable. I love to watch the TV show "Cheaters". On this show, a partner who suspects that his or her mate might be cheating hires a private investigator to determine if their accusation is true or false. At the end of the show, there is a confrontation, in which the cheating mate is suddenly surrounded by cameras and confronted by their partner, usually in an embarrassing situation. On more than one occasion, there were episodes in which one of the partners brought a great deal of money into their relationship, only to find themselves chasing down their half naked mate in the back of a pick up truck. During the confrontation, the same issues would tend to emerge for many of these cheating episodes: "After all the days that I go out and work hard for you, buy you nice stuff, and keep a roof over your head, you go and do this to me?" Then, the cheating spouse would honestly admit "Well, you did do all that work for me and provided money for us, but you were never there." This argument is usually being had while the "other guy" is sulking away with a sneaky smile, knowing that he has gotten someone else's benefits without doing any of the work.

In my own warped little way, I try to learn from shows like "Cheaters". One conclusion I've come to is that no one usually *intends* to hurt anyone else in a relationship. People might be selfish (i.e. wanting their cake and eating it too), but if they could be selfish without hurting someone's feelings, they would probably choose to do so. If someone were really trying to hurt their partner, then why would he cheat in private? If he didn't care, he would "do his dirt" out in public, where everyone could see. But everyone has needs, and each individual is fulfilling their personal set of wants and desires. What I also notice from watching a show like "Cheaters" is that each of us has different values. I am not justifying the actions of a cheater in a relationship, but sometimes, the person found in the back of the pickup (the cheater) may value time, love, affection or other things that the second partner is not providing. Whether cheating is right or wrong, one can agree that it is more likely to happen if needs aren't being met, or there are misunderstandings in the relationship. I am not referring to those who cheat just because they are greedy. I am referring to the reality that cheating is more likely to happen when needs are not being met. The person who catches their mate cheating (the "cheatee", in the example given above) may have decided that their financial contribution warrants their participation and inherent value in the relationship. Not that these contributions are not important, but it's ironic that they are working hard to pay the bills, but someone with no money is sleeping with their partner.

I must reiterate that I am not here to say that cheating is justified. Some would say that it's never justified. But the reality is that human beings have needs, and those who cheat usually do so because their needs are not being met within the context of their relationship. Many times, such a misunderstanding can be driven by someone who thinks that their financial contribution to the relationship justifies a non-commitment to any other part of the relationship: they ignore their spouse, treat them poorly, or don't spend any time with their children. They think all of this can be settled by paying the bills on time. I say these things from experience, for I have been the victim of unfaithful behavior in the past, part of it due to the fact that I felt that my relationship could run on autopilot while I spent time doing other things.

Given that you probably want to avoid the problems mentioned above, it's important to assess what non-financial assets you can bring to the situation. But the thing to remember about "value" is that it's *almost always* in the eyes of the beholder. If someone else does not see your contribution as being valuable or they don't appreciate it, then perhaps they are wrong for you.

Go on a financial diet

If you are getting ready for a wedding, you probably want to look good in your dress. If you are getting ready for the beach, you might want to work on that old six pack, at least if you want the women checking you out. Well, the same might be true for your financial situation. Not having it all together financially can be worse than having 40 pounds of blubber hanging over the side of your Speedos. You are forced to look in the mirror and see the blubber every morning, and you can't achieve personal goals because you haven't taken care of yourself financially.

Going on a financial diet is not just something to do for your potential mate, it's something that you should do for *yourself.* Like a good physical diet, it's not a matter of necessarily eating less food or eating things that taste disgusting, it's more a matter of making choices in moderation. The process doesn't have to be painful, and it can create a healthy financial lifestyle that others will envy, while increasing your own peace of mind.

I talk about saving money a bit earlier in the book, so we don't need to rehash this issue too much. But here are some steps that one can take in a financial diet:

1) "Stand on the scale" and see where you are

In other words: Measure your financial situation. Account for your assets, liabilities, spending habits, and income level. Be realistic and honest as you determine how you might look to your potential mate. Consider what good things you bring to the table, and the things that you wish were not there. Then, prepare to confront your weaknesses honestly. We talk about how to do this in our chapter on budgeting.

2) Set moderate goals for yourself

Start small. You don't have to change the world in one swoop. For example, if you overspend now, but eventually want to become an investor, you will have to go through a multi-step process. First, spend less. Second, save more. Third invest what you save. Take baby steps. Moving too fast can be overwhelming.

3) Choose a strategy and exercise regimen

Once you've set your goals, consider how you're going to reach them. This process involves baby steps, but you must always watch where you're stepping. That's where strategy comes into play. Think about the steps you need to take, and map out the strategy to the end. This allows you to envision the financial body you are hoping for.

4) Set up a feedback and monitoring process

Once you've created a strategy and put it into motion, you need a way to give yourself some feedback. This is where honest monitoring comes into play. When it comes to financial fitness, monitoring amounts to standing on the financial scale and determining where your body is. You are then able to assess whether you are keeping up with your financial diet.

5) Figure out your weaknesses and keep them at bay

If your weakness is spending, remind yourself of your weaknesses daily and avoid doing things that will cause you to relapse. If you don't keep track of spending, force yourself to create a budget. If you spend too much, don't take your credit cards with you. Whatever it takes to get your financial body into shape, you should be willing to do it. Don't let your weaknesses kill the results of all your hard work.

FINANCIAL FOREPLAY AND ORAL SEX

Twenty-nine percent of adults age 25 - 55 in committed relationships admit they've lied to their spouse or partner about their spending habits[6]

[6] http://family-law.lawyers.com/Stats-and-Facts-Love-and-Money.html

Maybe I am a bad boy for using the term "oral sex" in a book. But guess what? I am willing to bet anything that you already know what oral sex is. What's really funny to me is the fact that even though I know what it is, you know what it is, and most of us have thought about it at some point, we are afraid to talk about it. Well, let me be the first to break the ice and say, not only do I know what oral sex is, but I've experienced it! (Well, at least my friends have told me about it…..haha)

Well, before I get into anymore trouble, I'll start by saying that in this context, "oral sex" and "foreplay" are metaphors. There are no genitalia involved, and you don't even have to touch your partner in order to do it. But financial foreplay and oral financial sex can be both enjoyable and very important to the beginning of the Financial Lovemaking process.

I am going to describe oral sex as part of the financial foreplay process. In fact, I will give you steps you might want to consider to maximize your enjoyment of financial oral sex. But as in any kind of sexual encounter, creativity is almost always rewarded by additional pleasure. So, feel free to modify the process with your partner as you see fit.

1) Communication is key

By oral financial sex, I am referring to using your mouth in order to accomplish a goal with your partner. During normal sex, your goal is to achieve stimulation or climax. The same can be said about Financial Lovemaking. Just as communication is the key to good physical sex, it's also the key to great financial sex. You should talk about money, not as a taboo subject that you are afraid to confront, but as a critical issue that will affect your relationship. In the same way you might fear marrying someone who is not good in bed, you should have an even greater fear of marrying someone who is not good with money.

I encourage you to sit with your partner and/or with a financial counselor and just let it all hang out. Discuss everything from income levels, expected salary growth, money management techniques, and general perceptions and expectations of money. Communication can not only help you determine if someone is right for you, it can also help you determine how deeply interconnected you want your finances to become.

2) Sharing your financial fantasies

Building mutual fantasies is important during lovemaking. Do you dream of becoming filthy rich or just financially secure? Is it your dream to buy your parents a home or send your children to an expensive private university? What about retirement? Do you want to live in Mexico on the beach when you turn 65? Exploring your fantasies with your partner is stimulating because the mind reacts to some of our dreams and visions as if they are real. Take a second to think very hard about a very bad experience you've had in your life. Notice that your physical reaction may have been strong, as if it were happening again. Now take a second to think of an enjoyable experience you've had. You may have experienced some temporary euphoria resulting directly from that memory. The same is true for setting your financial goals and dreams with your partner. This is an important part of the lovemaking process, since it allows you to experience the highs of a financial fantasy to obtain the motivation necessary to set goals *together*. This can be part of your bonding process long after the thrill of physical sex has come to an end.

Verbalizing your fantasies may also help you to become familiar with your own desires and hang-ups. It gives you a chance to decide just how committed you are to reaching your goals, and whether or not your choices up to this point have led to the outcomes you desire in life. Therefore, not only does your relationship benefit, but you benefit as well. Given that a relationship is pretty much the sum of its parts (plus a little extra), you are making the relationship stronger by strengthening yourself.

3) Sharing your concerns and insecurities about money (and expectations)

Most of us have concerns or insecurities about money. Many of these reactions come from deep emotional responses developed during childhood. Perhaps you grew up without much money, so not having money is a constant concern. I counseled a woman once who was an absolute hoarder when it came to money. Her income was sufficiently high for her to afford a better lifestyle, but she refused to improve her lifestyle in any way, citing financial concerns. After talking with her for a while, I found that she grew up the youngest of 4 children, continuously fighting for resources in the household. The household never had much money, and she never wanted to return to the life she once had, so she would hoard everything she owned.

Sharing your perception of money with your partner is critical in order to understand one another. Your partner may have financial habits that make you uncomfortable, and it's important to include a strategy for dealing with their habits over the long term.

Even more important is sharing your expectations about money. How it will be spent, how it will be invested, and how much control each partner should have over the other partner's finances. This is critically important, since many couples can confuse themselves by not fully understanding how much their partner wants to co-mingle the family's assets.

4) Sharing your weaknesses and strengths

Sharing weaknesses and strengths when it comes to money allows you and your partner to explore what you can bring to the table in terms of money management and planning. If you are a heavy spender, you should tell your partner. If your strength is record keeping, then you may want to keep most of the family's financial records. You should also discuss how you are going to manage your weaknesses within the context of the relationship. It is your commitment to your partner that you are going to work to maintain financial security for the family.

5) Discussing how you are going to proceed with the lovemaking process

Talk about how you plan to share the bills. Talk about how you are going to divide the savings. How many accounts are you going to keep? Who gets to buy what? Think through every financial scenario, and you may even consider making plans for the possibility of divorce. Prenups can also be part of the lovemaking process, not because you expect to get divorced, but because you love one another enough to prepare for any eventuality.

6) Sharing your commitment to the process

Let your partner know that you are serious about making the relationship work, both emotionally and financially. Let him/her know that you want to improve on your weaknesses, and you are willing to put forth your strengths to the best of your ability. Make a commitment toward sharing in general, and also commit to financial transparency and openness. It is difficult to make yourself open and vulnerable when you may be used to being closed off and independent. Being connected and working together is a great way to start the Financial Lovemaking process off right.

GETTING FINANCIALLY NAKED WITH YOUR PARTNER

Twenty-four percent of adults say that honesty about finances in a relationship is more important than honesty about fidelity[7].

[7] http://family-law.lawyers.com/Stats-and-Facts-Love-and-Money.html

In any lovemaking process, nudity is always required.

Don't laugh, you know you've been naked yourself. In fact, I was naked not too long ago, since I do that regularly in order to take a bath. Whoever it was that decided that being naked (or discussing nudity) is a bad thing probably has some major issues. If anyone does feel that it's wrong to get naked, I would hate to smell their armpits.

Unfortunately, when I discuss being naked, I am not referring to taking your clothes off. While that would be far more interesting, I am discussing another form of "nudity" which can be just as compelling and challenging. Here we will discuss three types of nudity: financial, emotional and factual.

The three types of nudity relate to one universal concept: all illusions are removed, and the truth is revealed. One who is naked cannot hide behind magic tricks to improve their appearance. Getting financially naked implies that *you reveal anything and everything about your existing financial situation that may affect the well-being of your partner.*

Financial nudity can be a highly emotional process. If you think about it, you might realize that most people don't discuss money in their relationships until it's too late. By that time, you've decided that you've met your Prince Charming, and you fully expect to live happily ever after. You see the sexy eyes, and amazing body, but you don't see the yucky credit report, and 10 gillion dollars in student loans (yes, I said "gillion", even though I can't tell you how much money that is). You might see status symbols, such as a nice car, but you have no idea whatsoever exactly HOW MUCH of that car actually belongs to him. For all you know, 90% of the car could belong to the bank, while your partner has barely enough equity in the car to buy the front left tire. When it comes to automobiles, the debt usually outlives the new car smell.

It can be emotionally devastating to decide that you can't live without someone, only to find out that you can't live with them either. The reality of marriage is that you spend comparatively little time physically enjoying the person you are with, but you spend a LOT of time LIVING with the person you are with. You live with them when you go to the grocery store, when you are with your children and when you are planning for work the next day. Every aspect of your life depends on the person you choose to spend your life with, so it's a bit silly to choose to spend your life with someone just because you think they're cute.

Here are some pointers on how to proceed with getting financially naked.

TELL ALL OF YOUR DIRTY LITTLE FINANCIAL SECRETS

This is tough to do. None of us wants our "business out in the street". But I only hope that you've already put yourself into good financial shape (or at least better financial shape than you were in originally), so that your financial body looks the way you want it to look when meeting your partner. But if your partner truly cares about you, he will also take into account the sincerity you have for improving your financial situation in the long-run. The fact that you are reading this book indicates that you may be ready for a financial, as well as emotional, commitment.

During this process, you should fully expect to be ready to answer the tough questions. Bring documentation to support everything you say, and even consider volunteering information. Yes, this is difficult, but if your mate has any sense, they are eventually going to ask about the things you may have left out of the conversation the first time around.

Below are some issues that you want to discuss as you get financially naked:

1) Your debt levels

When discussing debt, you should have documentation showing all the debt that you have, including student loan debt, credit card debt, and any other debt you can imagine. Given that your partner may end up becoming liable for the debts you owe, you owe it to your partner to share this information.

Once you have your debt on the table, and have seen your partner's debts, you can discuss strategies for reducing the debts or consolidating them. You may find that your partner is willing or able to help in ways you may not have imagined. Let's take a look at financial nudity with the following example:

Mary and John, who are considering marriage in the future, have gotten financially naked with one another, and shared their debt levels. Mary, a doctor, has provided her husband with documentation supporting all the student loans she accrued during medical school. She attended Harvard, which is very expensive, so she feels that the debt is worth having. But given that her career has just begun, she hasn't yet had the opportunity to reduce the significant debt accumulated during that time.

John, her future husband, did not go to school for as long as Mary, so his student loans are much lower. However, he has $10,000 in credit card debt. This doesn't make Mary happy, since she feels that credit card debt is an absolute waste. Also, given that John has worked much longer than she has, she expected that he would have most of his debt reduced.

Making matters worse, John's debt accumulation and slow payment record has ruined his credit. He has a tough time getting loans, and he has bill collectors calling about the money he owes. This really infuriates Mary, since she has worked very hard to protect her credit score.

After some heated discussion, the two decide that they are going to attack the debt problem. Because Mary has not used her credit cards very much, she offers to open a joint credit card account with John that has a 0% introductory rate, saving the couple about $2,000 per year in interest. They then form a plan to pay off the credit card during the first year, before the introductory rate has expired.

John agrees to contribute some of his salary to repaying Mary's student loans, and he also helps Mary construct a plan in which he would handle more household chores so that she can have time to take a moonlighting position to earn extra money. This additional money is applied directly toward the repayment of student loans. While their troubles are far from over, Mary and John have found that Financial Lovemaking has led to a dramatic increase in trust and financial compatibility between the two of them.

2) Credit scores

Bring copies of your credit reports, all 3 of them, to the Financial Nudity session. Lay it out there for your partner to see. He should be fully aware of every detail of your credit history, your mistakes and everything that follows you and your financial life.

You may also have to bring explanations regarding why the report looks the way it does. If you have ever declared bankruptcy, that could affect both you and your partner's ability to obtain credit in the future. Your partner may have a lot of questions, and you should be prepared to answer them. Credit reports are tough to read, so spend some time learning what each section means. By the time you are finished discussing the report, your mate should be as familiar with your credit report as you are.

James and Sharon get financially naked by discussing their credit reports. Sharon learns that James has declared bankruptcy, and that he doesn't pay his bills on time. She is concerned with his credit score and poor bill paying habits. James explains that many problems began when he was young, and he continued with a series of bad habits that persist to this day. However, he's been working to change those habits and demonstrates to Sharon that he is making progress. Sharon is upset, but she loves James, so she is willing to work with him to help him improve his credit score.

First, they agree that getting married right away is not going to work. While many people might not postpone a wedding because of a poor credit score, Sharon feels that financial security is important, and in her mind (she doesn't necessarily tell James everything she is thinking), she would rather not take a chance on marrying someone who is not careful with his credit. But she gives him a chance to spend a year proving that he is going to correct his credit score. Additionally, they agree that because he is probably not going to see much improvement in his score over the next year, she would obtain some credit on her own when they were married, rather than immediately combining their credit history. Sharon knows that it would be extremely difficult to obtain credit jointly with someone who has not managed his credit score, and this is a source of concern. While James feels that Sharon has overreacted, he is patient with her and works to prove that he is improving his status.

3) Savings and investments

Since this is the person you are planning to marry, you owe it to him/her to discuss your savings and investments. This means anything you have that adds to your financial net worth should be provided, including trust funds, off-shore accounts, money under the mattress, etc. The level of financial nudity you choose to engage in depends on the degree of trust you have in your partner. The Golden Rule might be applicable in this situation, since you would have to ask yourself just how much you want your partner to reveal to you. In Japan, women have been known to save as much as 20,000 dollars without their husbands' knowledge, so at the end of the day, how much you take off in order to become financially naked is entirely up to you.

I must say however, that choosing not to be forthcoming with your financial assets can create problems should you ever divorce. Being dishonest about your assets during divorce proceedings can result in significant penalties and almost guarantee a ruling against you. In short, my advice is that if you have to hide money from your mate, it's probably not a good idea to marry him. Let's face it, what you're really saying is "I don't trust you", and you can't marry someone you don't trust.

When getting financially naked, I encourage you to bring bank statements, investment statements, and any documentation about trust funds or other accounts you may have. This will help you and your partner form a family balance sheet when the time is right. I will explain more about the family balance sheet later in the book.

Angela and Robert get financially naked by bringing together lists of their financial assets. They are each good savers, so they have much to bring to the table. Robert has $14,000 in his savings account, and $2,000 in his checking, with Angela having $17,000 in savings, and $800 in checking. This process helps them determine how much they have available for a down payment on their first home.

While Robert is a good saver, he is not a good investor. He has no money in his mutual fund, and no other investments. Angela owns stock, and has money in CD instruments. She explains to Robert that if he invests some of his money into a mutual fund, he would get a much higher return on his investment, one that exceeds the rate of inflation.

As a couple, they decide to continue to be good savers. While maintaining their current savings accounts, they commit to contributing 10% of their salary to a joint savings account for the family. They are satisfied with this arrangement, because it gives them financial freedom and security at the same time.

4) *Assets and Retirement Plan funds*

This is the part when you tell your partner about ALL of your assets, even those that are not liquid or financial (remember: a "liquid" asset is an asset that can be easily turned into cash, like a checking account or money market certificate). This might mean real estate you own, automobiles, valuable art, or even comic books. You should also let your partner know the details of your retirement plan and life insurance, assuming that you've developed that level of trust. Trust is critical, since we have all seen cases in the media about one spouse killing the other for the insurance money!

Bring any documentation you have about the details of your retirement plan and its assets. The same thing goes for life insurance. You will need these assets to determine how you will jointly plan for retirement.

I have counseled couples in the past who have very different ideas about retirement: one spouse prepares diligently, while the other doesn't prepare at all. This makes no sense to me, since it's the functional equivalent of one spouse expecting to be dead before the age of 65.

How your partner has planned or not planned for retirement may indicate something about their financial mindset. If she doesn't plan at all, and hasn't saved anything for retirement, this implies that she may be impulsive or myopic (short-sighted in her thinking). This might lead to problems for you. I know of a family in which one spouse withdrew the retirement assets out of the family account and spent them without the other spouse's knowledge.

Todd and Teresa (both 29 years of age) have become financially naked with each other. Todd has brought his retirement plan, a list of all assets, and the details of his insurance policy to Teresa's house in order for the couple to prepare for the next stage of the Financial nudity process. Teresa has done the same, but not quite as diligently. Her retirement plan paperwork seems incomplete, because she didn't go through the trouble of bringing all of it.

Todd senses that his future wife is not being forthright when it comes to her financial holdings. This worries him, since it implies a possible lack of trust. Todd wonders if his future wife is thinking, "What's his is mine, and what's mine is mine."

After talking things through, Todd learns another startling fact: His future wife has not saved a single penny for retirement. Teresa tells him that since they are only 29 years old, retirement is not critical for people their age. But Todd, who has taken quite a few finance classes, understands that retirement planning at an early age is crucial. He has "maxed out" his 401K plan every year since he started working at the age of 22, and is shocked to learn that his future wife has not done the same.

Todd feels uneasy and even betrayed, and he also sees his wife in ways that he never saw her before. He once saw her as a beautiful woman who would be good with kids. He now sees her as a possible liability in his financial future. He has a great deal to think about. While there is room for the fact that his future spouse is financially ignorant, this does not escape the reality that he now sees their relationship in ways that he never saw it before. They have a lot to talk about.

5) *Income levels and job details*

A critically important dynamic for any relationship is income. Money might not make your relationship a happy one, but it can certainly make it an unhappy one. Having a steady income is important. Your spouse should know how much money you earn. Your spouse should also be aware of how secure the income is.

During this portion of the financial nudity process, you should bring copies of your check stubs, and tax returns for the past two years (if you can find them). This will allow your mate to see how much money you earn and how much you've earned in the past. Your partner should have some idea of how much income you are bringing to the table, and whether or not this income is secure. You owe it to your partner, and you should expect financial honesty from your mate in return.

After you have the above discussions, you should have a long talk about your job, benefits plans, and details of your future with the company. Do you have a contract? If so, let your partner know about it. Does your benefits plan cover family members? Is there a chance you could be laid off in the near future? Do you plan to leave your job any time soon? Will you be out of work, and if so, for how long? All of these questions should be answered, along with any other questions your partner may have for you.

Shannon and James, a couple considering marriage, have engaged in the financial nudity process. Shannon has brought two of her check stubs from her job as a waitress so that James can see how much money she typically earns. She then tells him that her job doesn't offer any benefits, not even health insurance. She is hopeful that his job covers spouses, so that they are not stuck with high medical bills in the future.

She explains that her hours per week are not guaranteed, but since she is the best waitress, she gets pretty steady work. She also tells James that she'd like to leave her job and go back to school to finish her degree in accounting. Shannon warns James that she is going to be out of work for at least a year in the coming months, as this will undoubtedly affect their financial status as a couple. James is appreciative of the warning and respectful of Shannon's desire to improve her future. He considers the investment to be a good one.

6) Extra income sources, liabilities, lawsuits, child support, etc.

Not all income comes from a job. Knowing most of your sources of income is important, especially if your mate earns money underneath the table, or through some source with which you are not familiar. Understanding these sources of income and expense can be important for future financial planning. What's more important is that some of these sources may represent a risk factor for your financial security. Are you or your partner being sued? Is he likely to be sued by virtue of his profession? Does she owe outstanding child support or alimony obligations? It's necessary that each of you share this information so you can determine how you are going to confront and manage the risks.

Again, you should each provide documentation on all of these matters, so that you are both aware of the potential financial implications. If you have an unplanned pregnancy, inform your spouse that you may have to pay child support in the future. If you are behind on your child support, or your wages are being garnished, you should share this information. Yes, this is a "goody two-shoes" approach, but I've written this book assuming that you wish to begin your life together with nearly full disclosure and some degree of relevant trust. Given that issues like this never stay under the rug for very long, sharing the information now will keep you from having to be deceptive later in the process.

Michael, a physician, had some information he wanted to share with his fiancé, Jody. In the middle of planning their wedding, he found out that his ex-girlfriend, Angela, was pregnant with his child. Explaining this to his fiancé would be difficult, especially since she would want to know how another woman could be 5 months pregnant in the middle of their 2 year relationship. To make things worse, he recently discovered that his wages would be garnished because of an outstanding student loan. Additionally, there is a good chance that a former patient is considering a malpractice suit against him. The patient's suit did not worry Michael very much, since he is threatened by such suits all the time, but he felt that it was important to make his wife aware of the potential risks of being in a relationship with a physician.

Though difficult, he told Jody everything about the baby, the garnishment and the lawsuit. As expected, she was furious. But after having two days to think about it, and receiving a very sincere apology, she forgave him and they began working on a plan to restore their relationship. Of course the trust may never be fully restored, but she appreciated his honesty.

Regarding the pregnancy, Jody asked a lot of difficult questions: "Did you use a condom? How long was this going on? Were you lying to me every day during this relationship? Do you love her?" Michael answered all questions truthfully, continuing to express his undying love for his future wife. She decided that she loved him enough to work on a plan to manage their confusing situation. Jody could have just as easily left him, but she chose not to. For the pregnancy, they decided to attempt to set the child support payments before the wedding, so her income would not be considered in the calculation. They also researched child support statutes for their state, and figured out a good strategy to keep the cost minimal. Finally, the couple decided that the child would be a part of their lives.

Regarding the garnishment, Jody worked with Michael to find a credit counselor to avoid any other garnishments that might affect their income. Finally, she asked to see the details of his malpractice insurance, to ensure their financial security. She also checked the Internet and read up on his profession in order to understand the nature of what he does for a living. She wanted to be prepared for any surprises. Not being a fool, Jody only took the time to manage these issues because she believed in her heart that her husband's worst days were behind him. Well, at least 5 months behind him……or so he said. The rest of their story has yet to be told.

I am not one to judge whether or not you should forgive your future spouse for their indiscretions. I am only reminding you that when you lift up the rug, a lot of roaches can crawl out.

Not only are these financial roaches, they are emotional ones as well. The previous example may have seemed a bit dramatic, but that is the way life works. Financial complications do not arrive in a nice, prepackaged form. They come mixed with all of the other things that make us human. This is not to be taken lightly, for what you find under the rug can scar you for life and destroy your relationship. However, the same honesty you expect from your partner should be given by you as well.

7) *Throwing in the kitchen sink*

The final stage is what might be called the "Kitchen Sink" portion of the financial nudity process. This is when you share anything you didn't think to express initially. This is going to have to be done on the honor system, since it means that you have to share things with your partner that you feel he would like to know. Again, the golden rule applies, because when your mate eventually finds out, it may be devastating for both you and him.

The goal of this process is to ensure that you are "financially transparent". This implies that your partner can see your *entire* financial situation. Clearly, he or she will know whether you have an inheritance coming, how your family treats money, how you deal with relatives who want to borrow money, the works. You should do all you can to ensure that you have achieved a sense of "financial oneness", so you can move toward building your emotional and financial dreams together.

Some couples may enjoy a bit of mystery in their financial relationship. I am not sure if mystery is a good thing when it comes to money, but I am not here to treat you like a child. I am writing this section under the assumption that your goal is to obtain a complete merger of your financial situation. If you have another objective, then feel free to implement it in any way you are comfortable.

EXPECT THAT YOUR PARTNER GET NAKED WITH YOU

As you can imagine, getting naked is a double-edged sword: you have to endure the embarrassment of showing your naked body, but you get the pleasure of seeing someone else in the nude. The same concept applies with financial nudity, in which you have been forced to bear your soul, but doing so has given you an implicit right to see your partner's financial situation in full, honest form.

Given that the financial nudity process is partly based on the honor system, you may find that your partner is not as forthright as you have chosen to be. Of course this should alarm you, given that a person who lies about one thing is likely lying about something else. Beyond that, these may present early warning signs: either something is not right in their financial life, they are going into the relationship selfishly, or they are not usually forthcoming with personal information. All of these issues are problematic, since a person who has nothing to hide doesn't usually work very hard to hide things. Not to say that you should be overly skeptical, but perhaps some skepticism is called for, especially if you have been completely honest and open.

Here are some tips on how you can persuade your partner to get financially naked with you.

1) Expect (or firmly request) an answer to every question you ask

If you feel that a question is reasonable, then you have the right to gently, but firmly insist upon obtaining an answer to that question. Having answered the question yourself gives you that much more ammunition for the point you are trying to make.

Remember that not getting answers to these questions can lead to a life of financial and emotional misery. You might be uncomfortable asking certain questions, but you should ask them. You should also expect a full, honest and well-documented response to every single question you've answered yourself. This is not interrogation, but you should avoid getting meaningless responses. For example, if your partner is not interested in answering the question, you may want to eventually come back with another question. Listen to their explanation. If you buy it, then fine. But if he doesn't answer, then that should concern you. When someone doesn't want to share information, there is a reason. It either relates to the information itself or their personality. In many cases, it means that the person is hiding something.

You should ALWAYS expect full and honest answers to questions related to: Debt levels, income levels, potential legal liabilities, and credit scores. These issues are must-tells, mainly because they can affect your life in a negative way.

2) "Tucking fat in their underwear"

Tucking fat in your underwear might be something that someone does if he/she doesn't like their body very much. A person might get naked, and then try to hide their fat to look more appealing to their mate. Well, people can also try to "hide the fat" during the financial nudity process as well. Perhaps the credit report given to you is old. Or maybe the debt levels provided are an estimate, as opposed to a full assessment provided along with documentation. Now, these omissions may be inadvertent or intentional, there's no real way to know for sure. That being said, try to determine whether your mate is just telling you what he/she thinks you want to hear or omitting negative information to highlight the positive.

The same way you would not accept an AIDS test that is 2 years old, you should not take credit reports or other financial statements that are outdated. As you and your partner go through this process together, there should be a high degree of transparency, openness and relevance of the information provided.

3) Ask for recent documentation

Don't just take an explanation of your partner's financial situation. Ask for documentation. This is especially true if you have provided documentation yourself. Not to say that you should not trust your partner, but the burden of trust should not be placed completely on the shoulders of the trusting party. If you have already trusted your partner enough to become financially "undressed" in front of him, then he should be willing to get financially naked in front of you without fear of ridicule or rejection. That's true trust.

When you receive the documentation, I suggest that you make copies. I know this sounds extreme, but there are two reasons for this: first, you can always refer back to the information if necessary. Second, it gives you the time to truly reflect upon the information provided. Some things have to really sink in when it comes to financial information.

If it helps, try to make it into a formal process, where you simply trade information with one another or put it into a collective family file. At this point, there is no reason to think of your financial lives as being separate.

Check the dates of all items you receive. If they are not recent, ask why. Try to get the most recent information you can, since a person's financial situation can change very quickly.

4) Do your own investigation, if necessary

Yes, this might sound nutts, but you may need to do a background check on anyone you are merging lives with. Background checks are not very romantic, but think about how many people are taken to the cleaners and fooled by the person they love. They find out that their mate has another identity or lives an entire secret life that they knew nothing about. Many of us have seen the TV show "The Sopranos", in which the wife of one of the mafia bosses finds out that women are not exactly her husband's "favorite treat". In other words, the wife finds out that her husband actually has sex with men on the side. While this is an extreme example, the point to be learned is that people close to us hide things from us. There is no way to get around that fact. If the information could be detrimental to your well-being, you have a right to do your own investigation.

So, we have a choice: we can either stick to tradition and not ask the hard questions, or we can go through the process of confirming what we already know. You know your mate, and you know his personality. If he has been forthcoming during the financial nudity process, providing documentation and full, honest explanations of all relevant information, then a background check isn't necessary. If there's a bankruptcy or criminal record in his past, he has hopefully shared this with you. But if you don't ask, you may never know.

There are companies that perform financial and personal checks. Also, the Internet has a slew of resources you can use to find out what you need. But remember, being on the Internet doesn't mean the information is accurate. Also, there is the all important question: *If you feel that you have to do this much to get the truth out of your mate, is this person right for you anyway?*

5) Be honest with yourself

If you have engaged in the financial nudity process and it's been like pulling teeth, you might want to think about issues you haven't considered. This is a tough issue to confront, but it's very important. If you have a mate who gambles, wastes money or has not taken care of himself/herself financially, that is probably not going to change.

If you have not taken care of yourself financially, that's also something to consider. You should think hard about how your financial choices and personality mix with your partner's. If you're a heavy spender, and he's careful with money, this could cause major problems in your relationship.

If you feel in your heart that your partner has lied to you or deceived you, listen to yourself. Don't believe the hype. The consequences of bad Financial Lovemaking can stay with you for a very long time. Think hard about where your relationship stands and where you stand when it comes to the Bank of Love and Trust. If your partner has not made appropriate deposits, then you should consider closing his account.

DOES SIZE REALLY MATTER?

25% of respondents to a Newsweek poll think it is generally "Not acceptable" for a wife to be the major wage earner[8]

[8] http://www.divorcewizards.com/divorcestats_money.html

Size is one of those things that we have all asked ourselves about at one point or another. If we are "packing", we wonder if we are big enough. We then wonder if it's the size of the ship or the motion of the ocean. The general consensus is that there is no consensus, and outcomes vary from one person to the next. Another universal truth is that you can have the biggest ship in the sea, but bad motion can ruin things for everyone. The impact of size on intimacy, whether it's the size of a sex organ or the size of a bank account, almost always changes from one situation to the next. High wealth with poor money management is almost as bad as having no money at all.

The difference between financial size and physical size is that both men and women have to consider their size, and how their size affects their partner's. What's more, the size of your bank account can have a dramatic impact on the nature of your relationship, your power in the relationship, and the degree of volatility you might experience in your relationship.

Another point about size is that its impact can depend on your partner's attitude. If your partner feels that his financial size gives him an advantage, such an attitude can create hell for you. Additionally, if his wealth decreases in size, he can end up feeling financially, emotionally and sexually impotent. This is especially true for those who tie a great deal of their self-esteem to their level of income and wealth. There is the additional possibility that your partner may only be attracted to you because of the size of your bank account. While people never come out and admit that they are dating or marrying for money, the proof is in the proverbial pudding. Why do the rich celebrities date all the most beautiful women, even when they are as ugly as gold fish? How many old or unattractive Hollywood actors walk around with young pieces of eye candy? My point exactly.

Each of these factors has to be considered when thinking about how the size of your assets and bank account are going to impact your relationship. Here are some things about financial size you ought to keep in mind.

1) When size DOES matter

There are clearly cases in which the size of one's bank account matters a great deal. The first question you have to ask yourself is "how important is money to you?" It's OK to admit that money matters to you. I am not here to pass judgment on you. If, for example, you like nice things and your income is low, then size is probably going to be important to you. You may seek out a partner who can supplement your income and allow you to live a particular lifestyle. Below, I cite cases in which size may matter to you:

- If you are already well-endowed, you may not consider size to be very important. On the other hand, you may feel it important that your partner's income match your own. The expectation that your partner earns the same income as you is more challenging if you earn a good living. You may also want to take a second to make yourself fully aware of the tradeoff you are making. A lot of people date someone just for money, and find that they are miserable. There is more to a mate than the size of his/her bank account.

- If your net worth is low as a couple or you end up having financial troubles, this is a situation in which size definitely matters. Money cannot always make you happy, but money problems are certainly another reason to be unhappy.

- Size tends also to matter if either partner is extremely well off. Such a situation demands that you take your time when choosing who to merge your finances with. It also demands that you take steps to make sure that your finances are protected in the event of divorce. Those with extremely large endowments should work to rid themselves of the problems deriving from financial imbalance. For example, during the divorce of Britney Spears (the singer) and her husband Kevin Federline, I saw serious Financial Lovemaking problems.

Due to the fact that his wife earned several million dollars per year more than he did, the media frequently referred to Kevin Federline as "Mr Britney Spears". When they were finally divorced (which I predicted long ago, to be honest), Britney's allegedly iron clad prenuptial agreement was immediately challenged by Kevin. I believe that the challenge was due to the fact that most people are not going to easily let go of someone worth over $100 million dollars. Had Britney married someone with greater financial compatibility, some of these problems would not have existed.

The general idea behind the example above is that a wealthy person should be careful, especially if he/she is surrounded by people who struggle financially. This can be a recipe for disaster, since natural human needs for resources can make a wealthy friend look like a turkey dinner. I'm not saying that your partner is going to betray you, just that you should think carefully about how you handle your money in a relationship. Don't agree? Think for a second. Imagine that you and your family are starving, you can't pay the rent, and your mother needs surgery. Furthermore, imagine that your car is broken down because you don't have any money to fix it, and you are wearing the same clothes you wore 5 years ago. Now imagine that you make a friend who plays in the NBA. He has a mansion, two boats, five sports cars, and a sixty-inch television in his home. He spends $30,000 on trips to Europe like its nothing, and he can blow $3,000 on one night on the town. Would you be able to spend every single day with this person and NOT ONCE think about how easy it would be for them to help you meet the needs of your family? Could you have a best friend like this and never once let it cross your mind to borrow money from them? What if you were a person of low morality and the rich person mistreated you, would you consider taking advantage of the opportunity to retaliate against them financially? Lets' face it: if you are a person of means, others are going to have a hard time not noticing how rich you are. This is, I believe, the reason that most rich people only hang out with other rich people; because they don't want their friends begging them for money.

If your assets are substantially disproportionate to those of your partner, you may want to consider a prenuptial agreement. "Prenup" is not a dirty word, and it does not represent a plan to get a divorce. Prenups are simply insurance. This insurance protects you in the event that the love you hold so dear turns into disappointment and devastation, as it does for so many millions of couples. Many of our worst enemies were once our closest associates, and your life may not be an exception. Your spouse should respect your desire to get a prenup, and if they don't, then that's their problem. A second option might be simply clarifying before marriage exactly how the financial obligations are going to be shared. Does your partner expect that you are going to cover all expenses? When you dated, did he or she expect you to pay for everything? If so, then things are probably not going to change after you get married.

Speaking of attitudes, another way to tell if size is important to your partner is to analyze his views on couples and money. If your partner is well off financially, does she expect that this is going to substitute for other expectations of the relationship? Does she expect her spouse to stay home every day, or have dinner ready for her when she gets home? Does he feel that earning a high salary entitles him to neglect his spouse and not serve her romantically? Take a second to evaluate all these things, because whenever someone has a high income and is not yet married, there is almost always a reason. What I mean by this is that most single people over the age of 30 are single for a reason. Not that it's a bad reason, but there usually is a reason. It could be that they work a great deal and have never had time for relationships. It could be that they've been married already, or ended a relationship right before the wedding date. Or, it could also be something more sinister, like their inability to relate to other human beings, or the fact that they have an aversion to marriage altogether. I recommend finding the reason and acting accordingly.

2) When size does NOT matter

You should understand that there is a difference between having a high income and actually being *wealthy*. Also, there is a difference between being wealthy and having many assets. If someone has a lot of assets but debt to match, he is not wealthy. If someone has a high income and low wealth, she is not financially secure. A high income means that your salary is comfortable. High wealth means that you own things of value, and the value of these assets grows over time. For example, a home, stocks and a small business are assets that grow in value through time if they are managed properly. One final point to remember when measuring wealth is that having many assets, all financed with debt, is typically not a good thing. For example, someone may live in a home worth $500,000, but if they owe $500,000 to the bank, then the house is not really theirs. This situation is most risky when the individual is struggling to make the payments. All this should be kept in mind when determining the "size" of your partner. In other words, he might be "packing" in the front, but lacking in the back.

Size almost never matters when both individuals in the relationship have similar wealth and income levels. In some ways, financial and wealth compatibility makes the relationship simpler, since the matters of prenuptials, taxes and insurance can be simplified a great deal. For example, during the divorce of pop star Britney Spears in 2006, her disproportionate wealth, relative to her husband Kevin Federline, was likely the cause of the extended custody battles and challenges to the prenuptial agreement. Had she married someone financially compatible to herself, the divorce may have been less complicated. Similar wealth levels also improve the intimacy process, since additional wealth is likely to be created together. The obvious tradeoff is that it's sometimes easier to marry someone who already has money, rather than working to make your own.

Size also doesn't matter when your partner is fair. In such cases, your partner's treatment of you is the same, regardless of who the primary bread winner happens to be. These relationships tend to be incredibly comfortable, and indicate that your partner may be a secure, selfless individual.

Young couples don't usually have size problems. Size problems typically pop up for older couples who've had time to accumulate assets, obtain child support obligations, and declare bankruptcies. That's when the financial issues become complicated. This is also when the most questions need to be asked. For young people, the issues tend to be more related to existing habits and the direction their habits are leading them when it comes to their financial future. For example, overspending at the age of 21 means that the person may find himself bankrupt at the age of 30.

Does your partner have financial stamina, or is he/she a "quick climaxer"?

More important than your partner's endowment is the "motion of the ocean". Some people earn a great deal of money, but spend it so fast, it's as if they never had it. This is what I call a "quick climaxer". Depending on your psychological makeup, some people would rather have a partner with a low income who manages his money well, than to have a high income partner who spends like the world is coming to an end.

The main lesson here is that *there are not only a multitude of ways to measure size, but size only matters in the right context.* So if size is important to you, examine your partner's wealth, and how well she works to preserve it. Also, pay attention to how careful he/she is when dealing with business situations, since that can get you into trouble. Pay attention to the stability of her income, not just the level. A high income that is not permanent and consistent is not worth much at all.

Sandra had hit the jackpot. She was going to marry John, who was selected in the third round of the NFL draft. She and John were excited, and decided to have a child before getting married. This, she felt, was not only an act of emotional security since they loved one another, but it also served as a source of financial security. If John chose to back out of the marriage, she would still have a way to support her child and herself on a very healthy NFL salary. While Sandra was a good person, the instability of her parent's household made her very cognizant of financial security in her relationships.

Sandra was a bit worried about John's spending habits. He would go to night clubs and spend $500 in one night. He purchased a $100,000 car on credit, even before signing his contract. This made her nervous, but Sandra felt that perhaps she simply didn't understand the lifestyle of the rich and famous.

John ultimately signed his contract, and the two were married. The couple purchased a beautiful home on a lake in New Jersey, and she would watch her husband play on Sundays. The contract was for $3.5 million dollars over 4 years, which was more than enough to pay for the house, the car, and anything else they wanted.

What she and John didn't realize is that the NFL consistently signs players to high valued, long-term contracts, but the NFL is not always quick to honor those deals. Most of the time, unless a player secures a large signing bonus, the team is free to cut him at the end of the season, even if he's been a strong performer. That's exactly what happened to John. Although he was a very good player, he was not good enough to earn the $3.5 million dollar contract to which he had been signed. What's worse is that with so many young rookies coming out in the draft, many teams were reluctant to sign him for another deal. Before long, Sandra and John were looking to sell the beautiful home they'd just purchased, but their income from the sale was limited because they were forced to rush. John and Sandra soon found themselves struggling financially, especially given that John had *purchased a $100,000 car that had depreciated to half its value.*

The story of Sandra and John sends a very clear message: ***financial income is not the same as financial security***. Also, high income is not the same as a high level of wealth. Make sure you keep all these issues in mind as you "measure" your partner's size in the Financial Lovemaking process.

The situation with Sandra and John reminds me of a conversation I once had with a professional baseball player. He was not an All-Star, but good enough to play in the Major Leagues. I was just finishing my Ph.D. at the time, and he and I had become friends. I admired his new car, luxury seats at the games for his wife, and all the other perks that come with playing professional sports. I was just earning a professor's salary, and it looked like he was living a dream. There is nothing more exhilarating than to go play in a game in the afternoon, and then come home to watch the highlights from your game on ESPN.

During conversation one day, the ball player revealed something that shocked me: he actually envied ME! I was surprised to hear this, since I couldn't understand for the life of me, how someone in his position could envy a college professor. He said that in spite of the fact that he was making nearly five times more money than I was, his salary was not guaranteed, which made him very nervous. An injury or even poor performance could lead to him losing his job. Additionally, he was only going to be playing sports for a few more years, and then the financial gravy train would stop. He was not trained in anything other than his sport, which took up all his time. After playing ball, he would have to start over, go back to school and do something else. I could be a professor until I am old, gray and crazy.

This conversation with my friend left an impression on me that I would never forget. I thought athletes had it all, but I then realized that security and job satisfaction can be more important than salary. In fact, it usually is. This is a strong reminder of the importance of managing your life portfolio. That means income, salary and financial gain should not be your sole objectives in life. There is also security and peace of mind, which don't come cheap, but are incredibly valuable.

How does your partner's size impact the value of other assets in your own portfolio?

Remember when we discussed that the most valuable parts of our investment portfolios are not financial. Money is not nearly as important as our love, time, energy and peace of mind. Before getting excited about what a well-endowed partner is going to do for you financially, you must consider what they are going to do to the other parts of your portfolio.

One example might be a case in which your partner earns $300,000 per year, but has a horrible job. The job might require him to relocate on a regular basis, travel several days per week, and spend all his time at the office. When you finally see your partner, he may be too tired to spend time with you and your children. An individual that is obsessed with money can entirely miss the big picture in this situation. Raw ambition may lead him to feel that the obtainment of material wealth is more important than spending time with family. This is an easy trap for most of us.

Many spouses of doctors, lawyers and professional athletes have learned this lesson all too well. Their spouses end up living their own version of the show "Desperate

Housewives". Some women compete for the men that all the other women want, and feel they are the lucky ones, since they've had the chance to marry him. Then come all the other "perks" of this life.....a husband who is never home, who probably cheats, or even brings home a sexually transmitted disease. These "spoils of success" lead many women to have tremendous regrets when they get into their 40s and 50s. These unhappy situations don't just occur in the lives of women, men can also be disappointed when seeing their mates as meal tickets. For example, I would personally think twice before marrying a physician. Not to say that I wouldn't, but she would have a lot to prove to me when it came to her ability and desire to maintain a normal, healthy relationship. This is not, of course, to say that every successful person makes a bad mate, nor does it say that unsuccessful people are automatically better mates. It simply says you should not be "blinded by the bling".

I'm not saying that you shouldn't be willing to date and marry someone who is financially well-endowed. The point is that you must take a step back and avoid being caught up in the joy of having a partner who is earning a great deal of money. If a person loves you, spends time with you and is faithful, some would say that you've made a very good investment. In other words, the size of their ship may not be large, but they've got great motion in their ocean!

FINANCIAL MASTURBATION – ANALYZING THE RELATIONSHIP YOU HAVE WITH YOUR OWN BANK ACCOUNT

50% of women say that the earning potential of their mate is not all that important[9]

[9] http://www.divorcewizards.com/divorcestats_money.html

People laugh, smirk and get embarrassed when you say the word "masturbation" in public, or even in private. I've never understood this reaction, since a lot of people do it, and nearly everyone knows what it is. Put in a more generic context, masturbation is simply the process of self-stimulation. It could be viewed as a relationship between you and your own body.

There is also a relationship you have with your financial body parts, mainly your wallet. Size doesn't matter, since we can all enjoy our bank accounts, no matter how large or small they are.

The Financial Masturbation process is also most likely when there's no one else there to provide that stimulation. If you don't have a second income, you spend your own. You don't have to cater to anyone else's needs because the money is all your own. It's an emotional process that can provide some sense of climax as you buy those new shoes, that new outfit or that big screen TV you wanted.

The same way individuals have various responses to physical masturbation, there can be equally strong responses to our financial choices. The dominant concern is how our choices affect our ability to merge our financial bodies with another person's. If you have a strange or negative relationship with your financial body, this can, like regular sex, lead you to become a selfish financial lover, an unfilled one, or an unfulfilling lover to your partner. The love-making process must be a two-way street in order to be effective.

Ultimately, when we are considering the relationship we have with our bank accounts, we are walking down the path toward intensive self-discovery. This process involves asking ourselves tough questions, some of which we may not want to answer. But understanding yourself is the first step in the process of learning to please someone else. Below are some questions you should consider when it comes to the financial masturbation process. Feel free to add others if you'd like, since the process can be as kinky as you want it to be!

1) HOW DID YOU FORM YOUR FIRST RELATIONSHIP WITH MONEY?

You should stop for a second and think about where you first learned about money. Many of us don't remember our first experience with money, but examining these memories can provide clues about how we handle our money today. Usually, our first experiences with money came through our parents. They may have given us an allowance, or may have actually spent time teaching us about the value of money. We also may have learned from our parents by watching them. If you grew up in a poor family, for example, fighting for resources, that experience may influence your current relationship with money. For example, you may earn money now and hoard it, or perhaps you have wealth now and spend it on all the luxury items you could never afford as a child. If you witnessed your parents going through a nasty divorce with devastating and difficult financial implications, this undoubtedly affects your view of money.

Personally, my first relationship with money came from watching my parents struggle to make ends meet. My father was a hard working man, and always maintained some degree of upward mobility. I actually learned about investing from him by watching him invest the blood, sweat and tears that come from doing hard work. That's what drove me to move on to become a college professor, in spite of all the additional years of education required. My grandmother taught me about investing by giving me savings bonds for my birthday instead of toys. I didn't understand how something could cost $25 today, but be worth twice as much in just a few years. I also learned about managing credit from my mother, who explained the pitfalls of having bad credit. I didn't always listen to these lessons, but observing my parents and their own relationships with money influenced the relationship that I cultivate with money today.

The negative side of observing my parents' personal relationship with money was that I sometimes saw them struggle and fight about money. There were times when money was a source of stress for our family. You could always tell when my mother got paid, because that was usually when we had the most food in our refrigerator. My parents eventually developed an increasingly positive relationship with money and found their way into the "middle class". Right now, they are well on their way to planning for retirement.

Remember: there was a time when we didn't understand how money worked. We only knew it as the green stuff our mother pulled out of her purse to buy us a hamburger at a fast food restaurant, or something that could get us more candy. This source of pleasure became an object with which we had a relationship, and just like kinky sex, this is a relationship and frame of reference that stays with us forever.

2) HOW DOES DEBT MAKE YOU FEEL?

Everyone has a relationship with debt. There is a reaction that having debt creates within all of us and it's important to be aware of it. Sometimes having the wrong perceptions of debt can get us into trouble. But then again, certain perceptions can keep us out of trouble, but give us a boring life. The key is to know which relationship works for you and whether there are other ways to perceive debt that might be beneficial.

Let's revisit debt. We spoke earlier about good and bad debt. Debt also creates something called "financial leverage". Leverage is something you already understand, but perhaps haven't thought much about. As a finance professor, I think about debt a lot. Imagine being on a three foot long seesaw in the playground. You can't go very high on the seesaw, but you also can't fall very far. That's because there is very little "leverage" in the situation. "High leverage" is a seesaw that goes very high and falls very far. "Low leverage" is the opposite. Now, imagine a seesaw that is 100 feet long. The highs are very high, while the lows are painful…..you get the point. The same can be true of your financial situation. If you have a lot of debt, you are going to do extremely well if your investments pay off and your cash flow situation remains secure. But if something goes wrong, you are in big trouble.

Many people are afraid of financial leverage and avoid it at all costs. That's because leverage is risk, and some people understand that if you don't take many risks, most bad things won't happen to you. That is true; living a risk-free life is a great way to remain protected from failure, pain or disappointment. However, there is another side to risk. Most great American companies were created by taking a risk using debt and leverage, which allowed them to reach new heights. Had they not taken any loans, they would still be tiny firms struggling to survive and missing out on opportunities. That's the good side of leverage, and why it might be something worth considering.

Still, you shouldn't forget that leverage has a downside to it. Not taking the risks of debt seriously can financially cripple you for the rest of your life. Some people have no appreciation for risk and underestimate it. Many Americans use home equity loans and credit card debt as their weapons of choice in their quest for financial destruction.

Addressing how you feel about debt can help you understand yourself and your relationship with money. It can also help you reconcile your relationship with that of your partner. Simply acknowledging that there are other ways to look at debt is a good way to find common ground with the person you love.

Richard went to law school after getting his masters degree, and found himself over $150,000 in debt. This was not an uncommon amount of debt for a private school graduate, so he didn't feel that it was a problem. He figured he would take a job at a high paying law firm and slowly pay down the debt he owed. His parents had done the same thing, and he'd learned that there's nothing wrong with debt as long as you make payments consistently, and can afford the payments you agree to make. What's more, he was improving his life as a result of taking out the debt. No problem.

But he didn't expect to meet Jenny. Jenny had an intense fear of debt, primarily because she grew up watching her parents fight over her father's gambling debts. One night, when she was 7, she recalled seeing her father get his legs broken by some thugs who worked for the bookie who'd floated him a loan a few months earlier. To make things worse, she peeked around the corner to see the man put a gun to her father's face, threatening to kill him if he didn't repay the debts he owed. Eventually, her family fell apart, as her mother left with the kids when her father failed to complete his third term at Gambler's Anonymous. Financially devastated, her mother never married again.

Witnessing such trauma at an early age gave Jenny an intense fear of debt and its consequences. She didn't see lending as a happy process taking place between a customer and a grateful banker; she saw it as a matter of life and death. This did not make her comfortable. These views only strengthened through time, as she watched her parents struggle with the devastating consequences of her father's gambling addiction. This eventually led to her father's death and her parents' divorce. Her father's desire to take risk and borrow to make these bets eventually led to his demise.

Seeing Richard in such tremendous debt caused a problem for Jenny on two fronts: she was afraid of debt, and she was extremely risk averse (meaning she was afraid of risk). There is the old saying that "a woman's father is her first boyfriend", so seeing her husband up to his eyeballs in debt, for whatever reason, reminded Jenny consciously and subconsciously of her childhood. This would cause problems in their relationship unless they agreed to seek counseling. She and her future husband both realized that her aversion to debt was both a financial issue and a psychological one.

3) HOW DOES SPENDING MONEY MAKE YOU FEEL?

As we discussed in our section on Financial Masturbation, spending money creates an emotional reaction for everyone. This is because money can be seen as a source of pleasure. When you were young and saw the power of money, it probably left some kind of impression on you. As an adult, this may translate into the euphoria of finding a sale at the mall, getting a raise, receiving your paycheck or spending money to make you feel better. You may or may not identify with what we discussed earlier (about how you formed your first relationship with money), since your feelings about money could have been something that you've developed over your lifetime. Also, the way you formed your first relationship with money may not correlate with how *spending it* makes you feel. Spending can be an entirely different emotional process than merely having access to money, investing money or seeing someone else use it.

It's important to understand how spending money makes you feel because emotional spending can lead to impulse shopping. This is a bad habit, no different from emotional overeating, and it can cause problems in relationships. You get upset, run to the mall, and buy the first $300 worth of stuff you see, only to find that you don't even wear half of the outfits you purchased.

Understanding how you feel when you spend money can help you to control emotional spending. Knowing yourself is the first step toward controlling yourself. If you realize that going to the mall will trigger you to spend money, then you may want to avoid trips to the mall altogether. At the very least, you may want to leave your credit cards at home when you visit the mall. The reaction I am describing here is similar to that of someone who uses drugs in the same neighborhood and finds another park to attend when he is bored. When I found myself overspending, I would simply give myself an allowance every week, an amount that was comfortable, but I would then force myself to stay within that budget. In fact, I would only take one credit card and force myself not to use it. That was because I found that overspending was one of my major problems, and I needed to fix it.

Like an overeater who eats when he's depressed or bored, over-spending can occur for the same reasons. This is because the pleasure centers of the brain react to the new item you receive, or the power you may feel when you drop money on the counter. Spending money is an expensive way to make yourself feel better, and it may actually seem cheaper than therapy. However, it's not cheaper in the long-run, when you find that you're not prepared for retirement, or that you're destitute after losing your job.

The sad thing about the high from overspending is that it's like any drug: there is the low that soon follows. You feel that low when your pockets are empty, or you need the money for something else. You want to punch yourself out for not saving your money as you had promised yourself. You are feeling terrible!

But this feeling can be a good thing. It can serve as a reminder for the future. I encourage you to do the following, the next time you are feeling the low of overspending. Write down EXACTLY how you feel. Write down what you would've done with that money if you had it all over again. Write down a promise to yourself of what you will do in the future. Keep the list in your pocket the next time you get paid. When you feel the urge to spend, take a moment to read the list. Read it slowly and carefully. Then, close your eyes and take a moment to mentally revisit the feelings you had on that day when you felt like complete crap about overspending your money. If you're like me, your memories of that moment will be vivid. You might even start feeling the physical symptoms you felt the last time. That's your ticket. Remember the feeling you are having and tell yourself that you do not want to go through this again. Over time, your body and mind will gain a natural aversion to that feeling and avoid the things that cause the feeling to occur. There will be a cure for overspending, mainly because you will have felt the impact of hitting rock bottom. If that doesn't work, call Dr. Phil.

4) DO YOU FEEL LIKE YOU NEED TO HAVE MONEY IN ORDER TO HAVE FUN?

One problem I had during my spendaholic days was that I always felt that I needed money to have a good time. I would visit my daughter or my God children, and each time I took them out, I would bring $200 or more with me to spend. I would take them to race go-carts, to the movies, out to eat, etc. There were 4 of them, so that could be expensive. Just going to dinner in a half decent restaurant usually cost me $70, and going to the movies cost about the same. So, by the end of the day, I was broke.

Their mother was nice enough to tell me that spending money was not the only way to spend time with the kids. She mentioned that there were a lot of things we could do that didn't cost money, like going to the park or watching a movie at home. That was a good point, and I saved a lot of money by heeding her advice.

The same is true for you. One way to determine how creative you are at finding ways not to spend money is to go out for an entire Saturday and only spend $10. If you can't figure out how to have fun for the entire day with only $10, then that probably means you need to reframe how you think about your cash. Many of the best things in life are free, so I recommend spending some time finding them.

To get better at having fun without money, sit down with a piece of paper. Make a list of all the things you can do on a day off, with one requirement: that they be free of charge. You can add things that cost five dollars or less, like going to an inexpensive museum, or having a beer with your friends. But for the most part, try to keep the cost down.

Work on your list over several days. Ask your friends if they can think of anything to add to the list. Keep going back to it over and over again, trying harder each time to come up with a new idea. When you leave the house, keep the list with you, so that you can jot down new ideas as they come to you. Then, keep the list. Keep it on your refrigerator, so that when you're ready to do something fun, you can look at the list and remind yourself of all the fun things you can do that don't cost a dime. This can be one of the tools you use to help save money in the long-run.

5) IF YOU GET EXTRA MONEY, WHAT ARE YOU MORE LIKELY TO DO WITH IT?

There are some people who get extra cash and their first instinct is to save and hoard the money. They don't want to let it go because they may be afraid of what can happen if the cash is no longer available. For some, money is a security mechanism, a protective force, which is why they do not want to let go of it. They worry that if they spend money on a new pair of shoes, they will find a better pair later for a cheaper price. They worry that if they use the money now, they are going to run into financial hardship in the future and regret the fact that the money is no longer available. The list goes on and on.

You should stop for a second and think about what you do when you get extra money. What is the first thing you do when you get paid? Do you run to the bank to make a deposit, or do you run to the ATM to make a withdrawal? If you were to get $10,000 in an inheritance right now, would you consider that to be your ticket to financial security, or would it be your opportunity to have some fun and buy all the things you've always wanted? Seeing money as an asset is very different from seeing cash as something to spend. Seeing it as an asset means that you see it like a building, something you can add on to over time, and something that builds onto itself, like a growing tree. Seeing it as something you spend is like seeing cash as a liquid force, something that can help you feel better in the short-run, but constantly needs to be replenished. Whether you see additional income as a building block or a replenished object determines what you are likely to do with that cash. It's also a major determinant of the type of financial future you might be creating for yourself.

If you see cash as a short-term commodity that needs to be replenished, start thinking about how you can make it last and allow it to build. Perhaps you can invest 10% of every paycheck, or start putting aside for your first home. Is there a business venture you feel you can build with a small percentage of your take home pay? Anything that you put your money into that allows you to own something of sustainable value afterward is probably a good investment. Cars, clothes and other items are not usually good investments. Real estate, stocks, bonds, and funds toward your business or education are the best investments around. Keep that balance, and you should be O.K.

6) ARE YOU A DIFFERENT PERSON WHEN YOU HAVE MORE MONEY THAN YOU ARE WHEN YOU HAVE LESS?

We all know this person. The one who is humble and meek when they are broke, politely asking you to help them out. Perhaps they're willing to work hard to get what they need, when they really need it. But once they have everything they need, their attitude changes 180 degrees. The nice, humble person becomes the arrogant prick that you wish you never knew. She mistreats others, and arrogantly refuses to lift a finger to do anything, at least until she is broke again.

It's very difficult not to change who you are when you have money in your pocket. Having additional cash can make us feel confident, comfortable, and even cocky. If we have $80,000 in the bank, we are more likely to tell our boss to "kiss it" than we are if we only have $25 in our account. This is relatively normal human behavior. It's also something you need to take stock of. Some people become savers when they are broke, watching every penny. But they become big spenders when they feel rich. Of course, this is an illusion, because they end up poor all over again. Some people are the opposite, spending big when they feel that there is no incentive to save. But, once they have cash coming in, they are afraid to let it go.

At least theoretically speaking, the correct approach is to be the same person, no matter how much money you have. If you're a saver and investor, you should have the same mentality when you are rich as you have when you are poor. If you want to quit your job, you should plan while you are poor to accumulate the resources that will allow you to eventually leave your position. Consistency of spending and investing habits is one of the keys to your financial security.

This concept is what economists call "consumption smoothing". Basically, this means that you are not going from feast to famine, depending upon how much money you earned this week. It implies that you feel economically comfortable, even if you lost your job. It also means that you feel the same desire to increase your consumption without regard to how much money you earned this week. The additional benefit of having smooth consumption patterns means that you are steadily building wealth, which serves to insulate you from the effects of having a shocking decline in your income level. You have WEALTH, not income. Here are some questions to ask that will allow you to determine if you have smooth consumption:

1) If I were to lose my job tomorrow, how long could I go before I can no longer pay my rent?
2) If I needed to buy a new car with 50% down, could I do it at any time during the year?
3) If a reliable relative wanted to borrow $5,000 from me, could I loan the money to him without it affecting me financially or would I be forced to tell them to wait until I got paid?
4) If my car were to break down, and I had to spend $1,200 to get it fixed, would I have to borrow money or could I get the money out of my bank account without selling any assets, getting a loan or having to wait until payday?
5) When I get paid, do I feel really good or do I consider it to be just another day? Do I tend to have more cash in my pocket right after payday?

The answers to these questions tell you how good you are at consumption smoothing. Not being able to last long without your job, not having cash available in savings, or waiting desperately for each paycheck are signs that you can probably improve your consumption smoothing. Answers to these questions tell you how protected you are from possible problems, and they tell you how consistent you are when it comes to money. The bottom line reality is this: any person who earns more than they have to pay in bills, and has had a job for more than a year should NOT be living from paycheck to paycheck. Now, this is not meant to insult anyone, because that might be why you are reading this book. But the ultimate goal is to fix the problem.

If you are earning, say 20% more per month than all of your bills and personal spending put together, that means that within 5 years, you should be able to survive ONE FULL YEAR without having a job? Why? The math is simple. Assume that you earn $30,000 per year, with a total of $24,000 per year in bills and personal spending needs. That means that if you have a consistent savings plan, you are saving $6,000 per year. In 5 years, you should have one year's salary available. Notice that this calculation has been simplified to assume that your raises match the rate of inflation. It would take even less time if you a) are getting raises that exceed the rate of inflation, or b) are investing this money and earning a reasonable rate of return. The point is that living from paycheck to paycheck is almost always a sign that you can manage your money much better.

7) DOES YOUR JUDGMENT OF OTHER PEOPLE CHANGE BASED UPON HOW MUCH MONEY THEY HAVE?

We discussed earlier that size usually matters. But one mistake many people make is they put too much emphasis on the size of someone's bank account, as if this makes them a better person. This can lead to major problems in relationships. I have seen many individuals sacrifice their personal happiness in order to be with someone who makes a lot of money. That's not to say that money doesn't matter, but it's not the *only* thing that matters and it's not the only valuable asset someone can have in their portfolio.

Another thing I've noticed is that when someone with lots of money walks into the room, everyone tends to treat that person differently. In my profession, I've had the opportunity to spend time with people worth billions of dollars, and I've noticed that everyone tends to walk around that person on pins and needles. It's as if people think that by being extra nice to that person, they are going to get a cool million from his will. I'll bet that over 95% of the people who interact with billionaires almost never get any of that person's money. So, you can say that this kind of behavior is a bit irrational given the astronomical odds that a random encounter with a rich person is going to lead you into any money.

On the other hand, I have seen people treat someone differently just because he was poor. Sometimes, external appearances can be deceptive, since it's hard to get a pure grip on exactly how much money someone has. Bank accounts are usually invisible, and all people really have are "status symbols", which send a signal to others about the size of the person's bank account. Many times, the greatest status symbols are used by those with the least amount of money, or the greatest amount of debt. My belief is that everyone should be treated with respect, because you never know who is going to have something valuable to help you in the long-run.

Whatever your disposition, I recommend that you pause for a second and think about how you treat others. Ask yourself: if a millionaire were to walk into the room and speak with you, how would you feel? If you met someone who asked you out on a date, and found out that he/she had a low salary, would you be more or less likely to date that person? There are no clear answers to these questions, for there is no right way to deal with people all the time. However, becoming aware of how perceptive you are of someone's financial situation can lead you down the road toward self-discovery. It can also tell you some things about how you perceive money, and whether or not that perception is helping you to achieve your financial goals. For example, some people would rather seek out someone with lots of money than to realize how much money they could earn on their own. When someone else controls the resources, that person usually controls a great deal more.

The point of the above analogy is that, in the world of Financial Lovemaking, dating and marrying someone with a lot of money is never as good as having that money yourself. Having rich friends is not as much fun as being rich. For many people, having rich friends never makes them rich, it only makes them jealous. While I can't tell you how to feel about people with money, I can say that it's better to have the money yourself than to worry about the bank accounts of people around you. In fact, much of what you might think you see is probably an illusion anyway.

8) WHAT DO YOU CONSIDER TO BE THE PRIMARY USE OF MONEY?

This is an important question, since some people see money as something that should be hoarded, while others see it as something that should be spent. Some people see money as a source of financial security and advancement, while others see it as something to use for life stabilization. We discussed some of this earlier. But how you see money is not the same as what you think you should do with money. We've devoted earlier text to how you see money. Now, let's go a little deeper, in order to figure out what money is and how it should be used.

You can compare money to having a car. If you've got a new car, you can do a lot of things with it. Let's make a short list of the things you can do with a car if you were given one today:

1) You can drive it and let it depreciate over time.
2) You can rent it to someone else
3) You can park it in your garage and keep it in case you need it
4) You can break it down and sell the parts one by one
5) You can sell the car as a whole
6) You can use it to deliver pizzas
7) You can use it to visit relatives
8) You can give it someone you love.

This example shows that a car can be used for many different things. So, the presence of an automobile in the driveway implies different uses for different people. How industriously one thinks about the car determines how they are going to fare in the long-run. Well, you can take this analogy a step further. All of the actions and uses of a car can be translated into money. I will do that below. If given a pile of money in your bank account:

1) *You can use it for survival spending, getting you from week to week, with nothing to show for it in the end* (driving the car and letting it depreciate)
2) *You can make a loan and collect interest* (renting the car out to someone else)
3) *You can save it for later* (parking the car in your garage in case you need it)
4) *You can trade it for a duck, a new suit and a pair of shoes* (break it down and sell the parts one by one)
5) *You can use all the money for one big purchase* (selling the car as a whole)
6) *You can use it as working cash for a new business venture* (using the car to deliver pizzas)
7) *You can buy a plane ticket to visit your mother* (using the car to visit relatives)
8) *You can use it to help out a family* member (giving the car to someone you love)

If someone says "I have $1 million in the bank", what does that say to you? What do you think the person should do with that money? I encourage you to consider the fact that there are many ways to use the cash. Money is a tool; a means to an end. It's NOT the end in itself. I am not here to judge, but one good way of looking at the $1 million might be to say "Wow, if you make the right investment choices, you can help your family and also turn that $1 million into $2 million before you die, leaving a pretty significant estate for your children. Your children would not have to pay for college, and they would have a down payment for their first home. They would also be able to start a business and eventually turn that $2 million into $10 million."

There is no clear use for money in all situations. Many "financial experts" will tell you that money should always be used for investments. I agree to some extent, but I feel that an "investment" can even be something that simply makes you feel better. For example, a trip to Hawaii or a new outfit can be a good investment for your personal well-being. The key is to learn balance. If you are saving, investing and spending, you can have enough balance to have a happy life. Remember: happiness is what matters in the end. If you have all the money in the world and are not a happy person, you have lost the game in the end.

TYING THE KNOT WITHOUT HOG-TYING YOURSELF FINANCIALLY

Some studies have estimated that money issues are the driving force in 90% of divorces[10]

[10] Deborah Fowles - http://financialplan.about.com/cs/familyfinances/a/CouplesMoney.htm

You are ready to take the big plunge. Your heart races and the mere mention of your significant other creates both a big smile and a bigger erection. If you are female, then your response might be a little different (of course). You are in love, love, love. You would die for her, kill for her and drink the entire ocean for one kiss. OK, maybe I'm exaggerating, but you get the point. Also, I know that your "her" might be a "him", and your "him and her" could be "him and him" or "her and her". I am not one to judge, and I am a fan of love, no matter what form it's in. The point is that you are really into him or her, whatever the case may be. What's worse is that the powerful rush of pleasure created by the intense chemical reactions in your brain in response to this person's existence may cause you to end up putting yourself into a lifetime of financial misery for this person.

Many couples engage in massive orgies of overspending when it comes to marriage, engagements, and honeymoons. These are moments to remember, and you will definitely remember them every month when you get that credit card bill. Personally, I would rather remember with my photo album than my bank account. Not meaning to be a spoil sport, or anti-romantic, but the reality is that you might want to keep some fiscal reality in the picture as you go about tying the knot with the person you love. If you're not smart about it, you can end up tying your stomach up in knots until "death from the ulcer does you part". In other words, tying the knot can be tying the noose around your financial neck.

Think of it this way: you are not only getting married and showing love for one another, you are also merging lives. You're building and creating a future together. Marriage is the celebration of this plan to create, and you do not want to celebrate creation with financial destruction.

According to Onewed.com, the average cost of an American wedding and honeymoon is between $20,000 and $25,000[11]. That's not exactly "chump change", and it doesn't even include the average cost of an engagement ring. Add another $5,000 for some nice "bling", and you're talking about $30,000.

Consider this: for a couple with 40 years left to retirement, if you assume that their $30,000 would have earned a reasonable 10% per year in the stock market, this wedding would cost them over $1.3 million dollars in retirement funds. Translate that to 2004 dollars (getting rid of the effects of inflation), you're talking about $282,000 in today's dollars. So, inflation or not, this is a lot of money!

Weddings are wonderful, and you can have a wonderful wedding without starting your new life together with a new set of financial problems. Considering the fact that many couples argue and get divorced over money, it's almost as if you're increasing your chances of divorce by having a marital celebration. Not smart.

Here are some strategies for minimizing the cost of various aspects of holy matrimony. We're going to talk about the ring, the wedding, the honeymoon and the period after the honeymoon. Keep this in mind: your primary objective when planning a wedding is to have a great party, and to clean up the financial mess from the party as quickly as possible. That means getting out of debt, and moving

[11] www.onewed.com

forward with your financial future as quickly as you possibly can.

ENGAGEMENT BLING AND HOW IT CAN KILL YOU FINANCIALLY

Twenty-one percent of those who have lied about money to their spouse or partner have done so about spending on discretionary items like shoes and clothes. This is the most commonly reported type of financial deceit within relationships[12]

f

[12] http://family-law.lawyers.com/Stats-and-Facts-Love-and-Money.html

I recall seeing engagement ring commercials that encourage you to spend 2 months salary on your ring. After throwing up on myself, I would stop and think about how difficult it is to save 2 months salary, let alone spend that much on a single piece of jewelry. The diamond industry is pretty ruthless with its tactics, particularly with how they link love with the purchase of a bigger ring. "Show her how much you love her by destroying your self financially" should be one of their slogans. That would make an excellent slogan for a billboard. How stupid can they be? Well, I guess a better question is "How stupid can WE be?" After all, we're the ones making the purchase. We're the ones falling for this stupid belief that spending more money on someone for jewelry is a way to show love. Perhaps spending money is a way of showing love, but wouldn't I love you more if I spent money creating financial security for you? Wouldn't it be more loving for me to spend money putting food on the table, clothes on your back and creating educational options for our children?

Ok, enough grandstanding, I sound like the Pope. Let's talk about how to approach the purchase of an engagement ring. After all, it might make more sense to spend money on other things, but if you are a cheap skate on the engagement ring, you may find yourself sleeping with the teddy bear in the guest room for a while.

How about three weeks of salary instead? For a person earning $45,000 per year, that's a little less than $2,000, assuming that the person gives 25% of his/her salary in federal taxes. If you calculate the amount before taxes, it's roughly $2,596. That's not bad. I think that a man can save face by purchasing a ring for roughly this price. Not enough for you? How about saving for a while before making the purchase and padding on another $500 at the end? This has GOT to make most reasonable women happy. Either way, the idea that a person should spend $8,000, $15,000 or more on an engagement ring is silly for most people. Even if you have the resources to make such a purchase, the reality is that this money could be used for something much more productive. In the consumption-based culture that we live in here in America, such a statement is likely to get me into trouble.

What's worse is that an engagement doesn't mean you are married. If that were the case, then why not have the marriage first? The reality is that many engagements do not end up in marriage. According to the book "There Goes the Bride: Making Up Your Mind, Calling it Off & Moving On", over 20% of all engagements are called off every year[13]. Another sad reality is that even if you make it to marriage, nearly 1/3 of all marriages don't last past the fifth year. This means that if 10 people are engaged, 2 of them are not going to ever get married, and 1/3 of the remaining group is not going to make it out to year five. So, your odds are about 50/50 that your investment is going to pay off. That's one hell of a lottery ticket, if you ask me.

Think of it this way: If there were a stock you could purchase for $10,000 where the company gave you no positive return on your investment and had a 50% chance of going bankrupt within the next few years, would you make that purchase? Most investors would not, since $10,000 is a lot of money to gamble on a company that might go bankrupt. But let's look

[13] There Goes the Bride: Making Up Your Mind, Calling it Off and Moving On by Rachel Safier, Wendy LCSW Roberts, and Wendy Roberts, 2003

at the bright side. Your marriage is not just some fly-by-night company trading on the stock market. It's the love of your life, a person you expect to be around forever. Someone who has proven to you that he/she is right for you, who cares about you and will be there for you. While we can't forget that every divorced couple once felt the same way about one another, the fact is that many divorced couples should never have been together in the first place. Maybe they didn't spend enough time getting to know one another, or they ignored initial warning signs. But while we know that some couples are smarter than others, you have to listen to both your mind and your heart.

One initial thought on how to balance out your investment is to consider showing your love with more than just a ring. By putting a down payment on a home with the other $5,000 you were thinking about using for the ring, you are showing love and protecting your investment. If the relationship doesn't work out, you'll at least have equity to show for it. Ask yourself this question: If you were to divorce your spouse, and she had a choice between having a $5,000 engagement ring to "remember you by", or a home with thousands of dollars in equity value, which would they choose? The point of this question is to show you how you can spend the same amount of money and get firmer long-term results for everyone.

Here are some tips on how to keep you from being "blinded by the bling":

1) ***Save for the ring, avoid buying it on credit***

Starting your life with someone with a pile of debt is NOT fun. Remember: many couples argue and divorce over money, so by overspending on your love, you might be dooming your love to failure. If you know you want to marry someone, give yourself 6 months to save for the engagement ring. That should give you plenty of time to save and purchase the ring you would like your spouse to have.

2) ***Get the stone your partner wants, rather than choosing something at random***

You may luck out and find that the stone your partner prefers is actually CHEAPER than the one you would purchase on your own. It would be silly to spend $5 on apples if your partner would rather have had the 50-cent banana. Now, if your partner says that she would rather have a $30,000 diamond, all bets are off. If you can afford such high maintenance love, then God bless you.

3) ***Assess your partner's values and take them into account (bank account)***

Some women DO NOT like expensive jewelry, and consider it a waste of money. Not to say that they would not wear a diamond if given one for free, but some would rather take the money and make a more reasonable investment with it. Let's be clear: diamonds are NOT usually a good investment. Many times, you are paying a huge markup on its value, which will not appreciate when or if you try to resell. A financially-saavy spouse may recognize this fact and propose that the money be spent on something more reasonable.

Talk to your partner about the type of ring she (or he) would prefer. If she would rather have something less expensive, then discuss other alternatives for the money that can lead to your long-term happiness. Instead, your spouse may want you to use some of the money to reduce debt or make an investment in the family business. Getting a less expensive ring doesn't make you a cheap-skate, it makes you a productive spouse.

4) *Consider a two-tiered ring plan*

There's NOTHING saying that you can't get a better ring after you're married. Why not start with something you can afford, and promise to improve the ring within the next 5 years? Talk to your partner, you would be surprised at what she is willing to agree to, especially if you provide a good explanation. Have the discussion long before you are set to propose, so it won't seem so awkward. If you are expecting to have someone propose to you, then you might want to simply volunteer the information in casual conversation. For example, a person could make the following statement and avoid suspicion: "I think that couples who get married should not spend so much on their ring. It would make more sense to put that money toward a new house." Such a statement sends a message to your partner that they can hopefully capture and use in future decisions.

5) *Ask around and try to find discounts. Everyone knows someone who knows someone else.*

I don't recommend buying the first shiny ring you see in a department store. You should shop around, ask around, check the Internet, and negotiate like hell. Doing so can save you thousands on a ring. The only thing dumber than overspending on a ring is to overspend on a ring that is not worth the money. So, you should think of overspending in two ways: overspending for something that is WORTH it, and overspending on something that is NOT WORTH what you are paying.

6) Give more than a ring

If a ring arouses a woman, then a ring along with the down payment on your first home is going to make her just downright giddy. I recommend proposing with the ring, and then as a secondary part of the proposal, let her know that you have put together the funds for your first home together. This will not only enhance the quality of your investment, it will also make her proud that you're a financially savvy partner. If she doesn't see the value in this, then all bets are off. I am not afraid to say that you might want to consider whether your partner's values are in-line with your own. In other words, investing your life with someone who doesn't care about their financial future may not be such a great idea.

7) Pick a budget and stick to it.

Don't even LOOK at rings that are outside your price range! Department store rings always look so big, bright and shiny, especially in the special "ring bling" light they use. The light makes the rings look even more dramatic than they already are. There is ALWAYS a bigger ring, and they are ALWAYS going to try to sell it to you. They sell it with love attached and by challenging your ego. You are told that if you really love your mate, you will spend more. They subtly make you feel that you are not as much of a man as someone else who spends that last $5,000 on a ring. You see advertisements with the ecstatic woman, lovingly staring down the man who just bought her the diamond big enough to feature on the show "The Flintstones". It's clear: she is going to give him sex. You also know that if you want sex, you need to find a way to buy an expensive ring yourself.

Don't fall into that trap! Let's be honest: a good woman is going to want and cherish your love more than she cherishes some ring. Also, if a man has to pay extra money to get extra "lovin", what does that say about his ability to impress women anyway? There I go, challenging your ego. I will digress and move onto the next section.

8) Consider the "Cubics" if you need to.

Yes, I discuss this dreadfully taboo topic at the risk of sounding like a horrible cheapskate. But let me tell you a secret: many of the rich and famous people you see with the blinding rings on their fingers are actually wearing fake diamonds! Also, many celebrities are renting their jewelry to promote the products of specific companies. Think about it: you're the 8 millionth wife of Donald Trump. Everyone assumes that you are going to be wearing a rock on your hand with enough value to buy a small country. Would you actually WANT to wear something that valuable on your hand (assuming you don't have 25 muscle-bound body guards around you at all times)? Sometimes, the answer is "no". Also, if you wear the Cubic Zirconium, people are going to assume it's real because they know you are well-off financially.

I am not saying that you SHOULD consider a "Cubic", but I can tell you this much: many of the fake diamonds these days are so good that even some jewelers can't tell the difference. Also, there are now computer generated diamonds that even experienced jewelers can't distinguish from real diamonds. If you want to bling out of your mind and show a status symbol, then this is one way to do it without breaking the bank.

GETTING HITCHED WITHOUT THE FINANCIAL DITCH

Fifty-eight percent of newlyweds felt that dealing with costs associated with the wedding was the most difficult aspect of the wedding planning process[14]

[14] American express survey of 500 newlywed couples, 2006

There are few days in your life more exciting than your wedding day. Your mother is in the crowd crying, your father is smiling, your friends are gossiping about how rude and unruly your spouse's family is. They notice that your spouse's side of the family is drinking all the liquor and your spouse's side of the family makes jokes about how tacky the bride's maid dresses are. That's what's so great about getting married. It's a wonderful day, and a day on which we want everything to go PERFECTLY.

One potential consequence of having the perfect day is that the real price is being paid behind the scenes, after everything is said and done. The price of a "wedding gone wild" can be enormous, and set you back financially for the next 10 years. The memories from a wedding should consist of photos and videotapes, not old credit card bills and bill collectors calling your house. What would be even worse is if the marriage were to end in divorce, and you end up spending thousands years later paying interest on debt incurred to marry someone that you can't stand anymore.

There are ways you can have your wedding cake and eat it too when it comes to getting married. You don't have to kill yourself financially in order to live in marital bliss with someone else. Here are some tips below. Keep them in mind as you move forward, but don't feel that these are hard and fast rules. Ultimately, it's up to you to decide if the naked person next to you is worth the financial risk. But don't make this decision while your partner is naked, you'll only get distracted.

1) KEEP A BUDGET BY USING THE 15% RULE

Get your spending under control when it comes to getting married. If something costs more than you anticipate, commit yourself to getting rid of something. You probably don't need *everything* on your list, so there is ALWAYS something you can reduce or eliminate.

Set the budget according to whatever amount you can repay within 6 months of the wedding. I recommend you keep the wedding cost to 20% of your combined annual salaries. So, if you and your partner's total income is $65,000 per year, then your wedding costs should be maxed out at $13,000. I also recommend saving this amount if you can, and borrowing as little as possible. This does not include the cost of the honeymoon, so you have some additional leeway. Yes, this amount might be less than what your friends are spending on their weddings, but the reality is that many of your friends, like most Americans, are not making wise financial choices.

Put together a plan to kill the wedding debt quickly

Once you've created a budget, you should then create a plan for repayment of the wedding expenses. Such a plan might consist of the following:

1) *Using all financial gifts received toward payment of any debt incurred or replacement of savings used to pay for the ceremony. The remainder can be applied to the cost of the honeymoon.*

2) *Allocate 15% of all take-home pay toward the repayment of any funds borrowed.*

Assuming a couple has 40% of their paychecks withheld for taxes and benefits, this plan would take 86 weeks (roughly 1 year and 7 months) for all debt to be repaid. This does not include interest charges, so you should add a couple of months in the event that you are paying interest. My goal is to make a point, not to bore you with complicated or extensive calculations. If you want detailed calculations, go to my website to get a more in depth analysis: www.myfinanceprofessor.com.

Now, let's assume that the couple above was ambitious and made some modifications: they only borrowed ½ of the wedding cost (saving the rest), and then used 20% of their take-home pay, rather than 15% (in order to repay the loan more quickly). This would lead to complete repayment in 10 months!

This plan can help you put your wedding behind you and move onto married life as soon as possible. Wedding debt is NOT good debt. It's only good in the sense that it created the legal and moral contract of marriage, which is going to be with you for the rest of your life (I hope). But it's bad debt in the sense that all of this money was spent on a one-day ceremony! The point is that since the wedding day is only one day in the rest of your life, it doesn't make sense to spend the rest of your life paying for one event.

2) LIMIT THE NUMBER OF PEOPLE YOU INVITE

I may seem insensitive, but it seems that there are some people who are professional wedding attendees. They will go to anyone's wedding, anywhere, whether they know the bride, the groom, or the groom's cousin's sister. I am not sure what's going on with that, but quite frankly, it bothers me. Not to say that people shouldn't have the right to celebrate someone's love, but come on! Every additional guest means another seat at the reception, and another meal you're going to have to purchase. This is all done so that the person can have free chicken on the bride and groom.

If you love people, and want everyone on earth to share your day with you, I am ok with that. Some people can afford to share their wedding with the entire planet, but I'm not one of them. Well, I probably could afford it, but I choose not to do that. But if you are trying to save money, you might want to be clear about who can attend the wedding. You may even consider limiting the number attending to the people who've been explicitly written on the invitation.

On a personal note, I have a friend who is very well known. He was a professional sports athlete, and because of his stature in the community, everyone in the city knew he was getting married. It almost seemed as though the entire city was standing in the living room when he popped the question. His wedding excited EVERYONE, even people who'd never met him. He and his future wife, both good people who are reluctant to hurt other peoples' feelings, were stuck with a tough decision: they could get married in his home town and try to send wedding invitations to everyone who would get offended for not receiving one, or they could try something else.

The second option was to simply get married in the bride's hometown, which was about 600 miles away. The groom figured that this would serve as a natural guest list filter because only those who really wanted to travel to see him get married would go 600 miles to do it. Besides that, he was a traditionalist who felt that the wedding should take place in the hometown of his bride-to-be. But she had a better idea. Her family was from Mexico, with her grandparents, aunts, uncles and cousins all located overseas. They could get married there, and subsidize the travel costs of select relatives. This wedding option had the following advantages:

- Her poorer relatives, who could not afford to come to the US could now attend the wedding.
-He would be able to pick and choose which relatives came to the wedding.
-A wedding would probably be cheaper in Mexico anyway
- The wedding could also be connected to the honeymoon, since they would already be in another country
-They would be able to screen out those who weren't really interested in seeing them get married, while still ensuring that everyone received invitations.
-They would still get gifts from those who felt guilty for not coming across the world to see them get married.

The plan worked! The couple had a wonderful, inexpensive wedding, with their loved ones in attendance. It was on the beach at sunset, creating one of the most beautiful wedding memories one could imagine. After the wedding, the couple set sail on a 2 week cruise that took them throughout South America. Mission accomplished.

Here are some other money saving wedding tips:

- Have a reception only, instead of a full dinner after the wedding
- Find a discount dress over the Internet, rather than paying full price
- Buy a book on how to have a wedding on a budget. Follow the author's advice

- Have an early morning wedding and reception, since breakfast food is cheaper, while lunch and dinner options tend to be more expensive and elaborate
- Have an intimate wedding, i.e. the bride, groom, best man, maiden of honor and parents only. Then, throw a big party later when you can afford it.
- Make the reception either a dry reception (meaning, no alcohol), or include a cash bar. Often alcohol drives up the cost of a wedding reception.

HONEYMOON EXPENSES THAT WON'T LEAVE YOU CRYING IN YOUR BEER

A total of $125 billion -- about the size of Ireland's GDP -- was estimated to be spent on weddings in 2005. The average cost was estimated to be over $26,000[15]

[15] The "American Weddings" study conducted by The Fairchild Bridal Group. Fairchild surveying more than 1,000 brides

No matter how much you enjoy the wedding, the honeymoon is always the best part. That's when you now have the legal and moral authority to do your best jack rabbit imitations. If you're lucky, you'll rarely leave the bedroom during this precious time, as you consummate, consummate, and consummate your love, over and over again.

I'm a big fan of consummation, even when there's nothing to consummate. In fact, I think that you should consummate over a pizza or a birthday if you want. You should not need a reason to engage in such a glorious process. But you should be careful when it comes to honeymoon spending, because that is NOTHING compared to the way credit card companies may screw you after the honeymoon is over.

Here are some tips on how you can make the ecstasy of the honeymoon last forever, even AFTER you've received your first credit card statement:

1) SEARCH THE WEB FOR DISCOUNT TRAVEL PACKAGES

If you haven't been living under a rock for the past 10 years, you know about all the discount travel sites on the Internet. This is one of the largest industries on the web, and it seems like everyone and their grandmother has a discount travel site. Try your own grandmother's site and see if you can find a way to take the trip of your dreams at the price of your dreams.

You may even want to leave your choice of venue flexible, that way you can plan your trip for the nicest place you can travel to at a reduced fare. Why does this work best? Because airline and travel prices tend to be based on something economists call "elasticity of consumption". Basically, elasticity represents how much you care or don't care about doing the thing you are trying to do. For example, senior citizens get the best movie prices, especially if they are attending during the day. On the other hand, teenagers, who usually attend at night, get the worst prices. Why do you think that is? It's because teenagers would probably go to the movies even if the tickets were $25 each. Teenagers have a date, and they're going to go on that date. On the other hand, a senior citizen can take it or leave it. In other words, the market for teenagers is *inelastic* (they really need what you are selling), and the market for senior citizens is highly *elastic* (they can walk away much easier, and their demand for the product is much more flexible than other groups).

The same is true for airline travel. Business passengers have the least elasticity in their demand, meaning many of them will travel at almost any cost. If they've got to make a deal, they are going to find a way to travel and make the deal. I had to do a TV show on a major network once, and the show was on a timely topic. In order to get me to the studio, the producers of the show booked the ticket in the morning, flew me out in the afternoon, and flew me back that evening. The ticket price was much higher than if they'd booked the ticket well in advance with flexible travel dates. But with the millions in revenue the show generated every night, their goal was not to save money on plane tickets, it was to have a great show. So, their demand was highly inelastic (like the teenager's demand for a movie ticket).

You can use elasticity to your advantage when traveling. Every option you have should be as flexible as possible: travel dates, travel times, airline and travel destination. This can help you save a bundle on your vacation plans. Not everyone can be this flexible, but if there is flexibility in your travel plans (at least to the point of planning well in advance), use that flexibility to your advantage.

2) ASKS YOUR GUESTS TO CONTRIBUTE TO THE COST

There is nothing wrong with asking for cash at your wedding. It's your day, you should get what you want.

3) GO TO YOUR HONEYMOON DESTINATION OFF-SEASON

If you are looking for adventure, why not go to some exotic location off-season? That would allow you to experience something new and save a bundle in the process. It would also be less-crowded and perhaps more enjoyable.

4) DO YOU HAVE FREQUENT FLIER MILES?

If you have frequent flier miles, use them liberally. It can significantly impact the cost of the trip. But with frequent flier programs changing, getting the ticket you want, when you want, can make life that much more complicated. So, I recommend attempting to use your miles, but ensuring that you put the elasticity concept into full-effect: Be as flexible as you can when it comes to time, destination, and perhaps even airline, and you might find this to be a great way to save money.

5) AGAIN: SET A HONEYMOON BUDGET

Budgeting should be a part of everything you do. Little extras can completely ruin your bank account, and you should be especially careful of these extras during the honeymoon. When you start the planning process, give yourself plenty of elbow room to afford everything you want, but be sure to set your limit well in advance. Also, put aside extra cash for incidentals, since incidentals are always the fudge factor that destroys whatever budget we might have had in place.

6) FLY IN THE MIDDLE OF THE WEEK

Most people fly on the weekends, so if you are able to take a day or two off work and fly during the middle of week, you are likely to save a ton of money.

7) FIND A PACKAGE

Make it worth the travel agent's while to get you the best price possible. You can do this by ordering a package.

Hammering the point home

Just to make a final point, I am going to pull out some quick and dirty financial wizardry to show you exactly how much your spending on the honeymoon, ring and wedding ceremony can set you back financially. If you think I am belaboring the point, the answer is yes. I am doing this because the point is *that* important, and in the event that you did not understand the financial impact of wedding costs from my prior example, I will include another for good measure. This example shows how your wedding spending doesn't just affect your bank account now, it also affects your retirement. Money that you spend getting married could be saved and invested for your financial future, so by overspending, you are not only losing money today, you are losing the growth on that money which is going to occur tomorrow.

Assume that you are 25 years old, and you spend $10,000 on your ring, $25,000 on your wedding, and $10,000 on your honeymoon. How much do you think this is going to affect your retirement at the age of 65? Well, if you assume that the stock market grows at 10%, which is quite reasonable, you would lose a little over $2 million in your retirement portfolio. If you are 35, you lose $785,000. You lose less if you are older because your money has less time to grow. The key point is that you are losing big if you plan too big on your wedding date. Two "20-somethings" can add another million to their retirement by using the funds for something more productive, such as the down payment for a home. That's as honest and as real as it gets.

AFTER THE HONEYMOON IS OVER

Couples that hold "destination weddings" (getting married in a place away from their home towns) spend 41% less than couples in conventional weddings[16]

[16] The "American Weddings" study conducted by The Fairchild Bridal Group. Fairchild surveyed more than 1,000 brides

You're finally home after all the excitement. You have a living room full of stuff that has been mailed to you, you've had more sex than a human being is supposed to have in such a short time, and you've finished sending out all the thank you cards. What do you do now? Well, this is the time to get your financial future started off right. This is when you snap yourself out of the marital bliss, and take advantage of the fact that you are now starting your lives together with a head start. You have a set of wedding gifts and hopefully a ton of cash in the bank. There is no better time than the present to get your marital Financial Lovemaking process off on the right foot.

Here are some things you should do IMMEDIATELY after the wedding is over:

1) CREATE A PLAN ON PAPER TO GET RID OF ALL WEDDING DEBTS AS SOON AS POSSIBLE.

We discussed such plans earlier in the book. Write one that works for you and start implementing the plan immediately.

2) DOCUMENT A CLEAR SAVING, INVESTMENT AND BILL PAYING PLAN

We discussed savings and investment plans earlier. These should be implemented immediately after you've put together a plan to rid yourself of all wedding related debt.

3) SET FINANCIAL GOALS

Goals should be set for 6, 12, 36 and 60 months. Then, there should be a category called "Long-term goals", which has an indefinite time period associated with it. Setting these goals and putting them down on paper will give you a focal point, something that reminds you of what your organizational objective is. Yes, it sounds strange to call your marriage an organization, but really you are a team. You are trying to achieve things together, so you should have a joint focus. Setting goals helps to create that.

4) REVIEW YOUR RETIREMENT AND BENEFITS PLANS

Make sure there are minimal redundancies in health insurance. Check your retirement plans. Have the administrator of your retirement plan do a projection to ensure that you're going to have enough money when you get older. Make sure that you have all that you need in case of health emergencies, death or other negative eventualities. Your lives have changed, so you have to structure your current life around your new one. Putting things off until the highly ambiguous "eventually" is a good way to find yourself hamstrung by a surprise event in your life.

5) WRITE OR REVIEW WILLS AND ESTATE PLANS

Everyone should have a will. If you don't, you're asking for trouble. If you die without leaving your money to anyone, the government (and the IRS) get to decide what to do with your assets. What's worse is that by the time the government is done shelling out the money for your expenses, and they finally get around to your loved ones, many of your most precious assets will be sold away. Your loved ones will have long suffered through the problems that come with not having enough cash to meet their immediate needs. The quickest way to break up an estate is to die without a will. Make sure you write one. Go to www.myfinanceprofessor.com to learn how to write a will.

6) DO A FAMILY BALANCE SHEET

A family balance sheet helps you figure out how much you're worth as a couple. It helps you assess where you are right now and see where it is you want to go. There are technical ways to put together a balance sheet, but I am going to give you a simple format:

On the left side of a balance sheet, you should list every asset you own. That means your car, house, jewelry, investments, savings and checking accounts, retirement accounts, etc. List their fair market value, essentially what you think you could get if you were to sell them on Ebay or some other auction site. What does that mean? Well, that means that your record collection might not have as much financial value as it has sentimental value! You may have to get your home appraised, but you can use a rough estimate if you wish. This doesn't have to be a precise procedure, it should be as precise as you and your spouse feel it needs to be. Also, include as assets any money that's owed to you, say, from a pending lawsuit that you just won, or money owed to you by a friend (only list debt from friends if you feel you are definitely going to get it back). Basically, you should list everything you own of value. If you have your own business, give it a careful valuation. I recommend using the following simple procedure to appraise the value of your business:

List the amount you earned this year in total revenue. Multiply it by 10. Use this as the value of your business. It should be noted that this procedure is incredibly imprecise. However, it's simple and gives you a rough estimate of the value of your company, even if your company is almost 100% debt. The goal is not to create a perfect valuation of your assets. Rather, it is to get a solid estimate of where you stand financially.

On the right hand side of the balance sheet, list all of your debts: all credit card debt, car loans, student loans, mortgage debt, and anything else you owe. Some people include debt from the next year's rent, utilities, etc, but I don't think that's necessary. After all, much of that is going to be taken care of by your salary from the following year anyway. Basically, anything you owe anyone should be included on the right hand side of this sheet.

Add up the total from the left hand side of the sheet (the assets side). Add up the total from the right hand side of the sheet (the liabilities side). Subtract the difference between the two numbers. If the assets side is greater than the liabilities side, you have a positive net worth. Another way of saying this is that you are "solvent". If the liabilities exceed the assets, you are "insolvent". Hopefully you're solvent, but even if you are not, you have now taken the first step toward fixing the problem.

Sample balance sheet

Assets			Liabilities		
Car	$	10,000	Student Loans	$	75,000
House	$	100,000	Mortgage	$	82,000
stocks	$	25,000	Credit cards	$	6,000
furniture	$	5,000	Owed to my mother	$	3,000
baseball cards	$	5,000			
retirement plan	$	75,000			
Cash in bank	$	4,000			
Savings account	$	10,000			
Total Assets	$	234,000	Total Liabilities	$	166,000
Assets - Liabilities	$	68,000			

In the above example, notice that the person has a positive net worth of $68,000. This means that when they add up everything they own and subtract all that they owe, they have a difference of $68,000. Therefore, they are solvent.

Also, notice in this example that the numbers are not calculated down to the penny. Most of the numbers are rough estimates, designed to give the person some idea of where they stand financially.

Finally, notice that the entire value of the house is put on the asset side of the balance sheet, even though they still owe $82,000 on the mortgage. This balances out, so that $18,000 ($100,000 - $82,000) is contributed to their net worth by the value of the home.

7) CREATE A FAMILY INCOME STATEMENT

A family income statement is not like the balance sheet. The balance sheet is a snapshot of where you are as a family. The income statement is more of a "flowing measure" (think of water flowing into a bucket) of where you are going. You can call it a flow because your income in the future flows into your assets, and your assets grow because of the income that has been put into them. So, basically, your income says a lot about how your financial position changes through time.

Again, there are more complicated ways to set up an income statement, but I'm going to keep it simple. I keep things simple so people can get an idea of where they are without having to go through a bunch of ridiculous calculations. Broke people usually know they're broke, so there is no point in pulling out a microscope to show them that.

To create an income statement, do the following: List your gross income. Do NOT list your take-home pay, because it can be misleading. You should look at what you have before taxes, life insurance, health insurance and everything else is taken out. After you list your gross income, you should list all anticipated expenses. Expenses include any and everything you expect to spend money on: rent, utilities, car payments, food, entertainment, clothing, bus passes, etc. List *every single expense you have.* Calculate the difference between the two to get your cash surplus. If your surplus is positive, that's a good thing. Hopefully, you're going to have plenty of money to save. If it's negative, you're going to have to borrow to meet your basic needs. That can be a bad thing.

You can do your income projections either monthly or annually, whichever you are comfortable with. The idea behind this statement is to get some understanding of the future cash flow needs of your family. You can look into the future and make modifications to help you get where you want to be financially.

8) READ A BOOK TOGETHER

Choose a topic, any topic. The book might be something that teaches you how to manage your money better, how to enhance your sex life, or how to manage your relationship. Basically, reading something from the outside together will help you learn how to *remain* married. This is critical for a couple of reasons: First, marriage is not about being together, it's about *growing together*. Two trees that are brought together have spent their entire lives growing in their own way. Their branches take whatever direction they want to go, and the likelihood of perfectly fitting with another tree is very low, since the branches will cross one another and not fit. If neither tree grows in sync with the other, they cannot remain side by side.

But, if the two trees agree to grow together, as much as possible, eventually the new growth will overshadow the old, and the two trees eventually become one. Becoming one increases the likelihood that the trees can continue their growth and existence in a comfortable fashion.

You should consider reading the book together to be a way to protect your investment. Seriously. Why invest so much of your portfolio in this marriage if you aren't going to make it work? There are so many self-help books on marriage, it's ridiculous. Find one and read it together, then talk about it.

CHECKING THE FINANCIAL GENETICS IN THE FINANCIAL LOVE-MATING PROCESS (AFTER ALL, EVERYTHING IS RELATIVE)

The average American was planning to spend $907 at Christmas in 2006[17]

[17] American Research Group survey, 2006

Many individuals seem to live in a beautiful and dramatically designed vacuum. They think that THE world is THEIR world, and that nothing else in the world matters. When discussions on family and friends are had, the focus turns back to the individual, as if they are the only ones who are important.

In some cases, it may be safe to assume that the individual is completely and clearly distinct from the family. Some people only see or interact with relatives every few months, and when they do, it's as if they are not related. But most people don't behave this way. They are eternally connected to their siblings, parents, and even cousins, nieces and nephews. These connections are part of what make us human. These connections are also critical to understanding and analyzing our relationships with other people. If the individual with whom you are going to spend the remainder of your life has an odd or unhealthy relationship with the people they loved before they met you, this can lead to the destruction of your relationship.

Given that this book is about finance, we can focus on the financial relationships you or your partner may have with other people. These relationships can be complex, because many families feel that it's each member's obligation to take care of everyone else in the family. In some cases, there may be children who feel that it's the parents' job to pay for everything, or there may be deadbeat relatives who continuously prey on those who are more financially secure. There may be huge debts shared between relatives, parents taking care of their children as if they are welfare recipients, or ailing parents posing a tremendous financial strain on their children. Not that taking care of family is a bad thing to do. It's simply something that should be considered so that you know what you are getting into.

All these factors should be analyzed in the Financial Lovemaking process. Don't ignore unhealthy financial relationships or assume that they are going to change just because you've decided to tie the knot. The best assumption to make is that what you see is what you are going to get. Any promises made to change preexisting relationships are not likely to be kept. Even if your significant other promises to change the unhealthy relationship he has with his baby sister, chances are that the relationship is going to remain the same. This is due to the fact that your mate has an incredibly complicated relationship with his sister that even he doesn't understand. Not to mention that he has known his little sister for his entire life, and only known you for a short time. If he doesn't understand the nature of his relationship, then how in the world are you going to come in from the outside and change it?

Examples of potentially unhealthy pre-existing relationships between family members:

Situation 1: *You are upset because your fiancé is always giving money to his brother.*

His Explanation: *"Well, I had to loan my brother the money because he doesn't have a job right now."*

The truth: *"My brother is always going through some kind of financial emergency, and I am always the one willing to bail him out of it."*

Situation 2: *Your spouse wants her parents to come live with you.*

Explanation: *"My parents are going to come live with me for a little while, until they get on their feet."*

The truth: *"My parents are getting older, so if they can't get on their feet now, they probably never will."*

Situation 3: *Your spouse's sister is asking for money to help with her situation.*

Explanation: *"My sister is having trouble with the kids right now, and just needs money until she gets paid."*

The truth: *"My sister never pays me back because she expects her older brother to protect her as she did when we were young."*

The list can go on and on. It's not to say that these relationships are wrong, or that everyone who presents an explanation is lying to you. It's to say that pre-existing financial commitments are going to provide additional strain on your partner's ability to make financial love with you. It's no different from sex: if your partner's attention is elsewhere, he/she has a decreased ability to keep you satisfied. Unless, perhaps, they are well-endowed enough to satisfy multiple partners!

Another thing to remember is that old habits are hard to break. A partner may promise that he or she won't continue to help a free-loading relative, but there is an equally strong likelihood that your disapproval is only going to cause your partner to lie to you about their financial decisions.

Below I provide some thoughts and suggestions on how you can manage the family interaction so that you at least know what you are getting into. Study these tips carefully, for they can help you avoid a great deal of strain in the long-run!

I. OBSERVE, OBSERVE, OBSERVE

When you're invited to family gatherings, check out the family you're marrying into. Pay attention to how each family member interacts with the others. Talk to them individually, and do more listening than talking. Get a feel for how they deal with one another, how close they are, and whether there are any "black sheep" in the family. Usually the black sheep of the family is the financial black sheep as well. Many families have a black sheep, and I hope your partner is not that person! But if your partner is the black sheep of the family, you should seriously ask yourself why that is. If you don't have a problem with the fact that your partner is considered the black sheep of the family, just make sure you're not getting fleeced!

Other important things you might want to observe:

- What are the financial habits of the members of your partner's family?

- What kind of lifestyle does your partner's family live, and does it fit with their income level?

- Is each member of the family relatively independent or continuously coming back to the family for resources?

- Have the parents of the household reinforced financial responsibility to the children? Are the children heeding those lessons and exhibiting them through principles such as home ownership, or continued saving and investing of personal resources?

- Do they feel the need to "keep up with the Jones' " by living a life that they cannot afford?

Martha was hesitant about marrying into Jerry's family. Jerry was a successful attorney, but it appeared that he was the only financially successful person in his family. His relatives seemed to realize this also, since every financial burden placed on the family seemed to fall right onto Jerry's shoulders. Before deciding to have a family, these burdens were not particularly problematic. As a free-spending bachelor, Jerry had no problem paying his mother's mortgage in spite of his father's gambling problem. He was also able to take care of his sister's children once she became hooked on drugs and spent most of her time in the street.

Jerry's father's gambling problem also worried Martha. She was concerned that his father's gambling set a bad example for Jerry, since Jerry was also known to frequent the casino weekly and spend several hundred dollars in cash at the tables. In spite of his six figure salary, Jerry was usually broke and had no savings to speak of. Additionally, she saw Jerry and his family spending any large sum of cash quickly. They'd buy new toys and clothes for the children, go to nice restaurants or take expensive trips. Never once was there any consideration for using the money as a down payment on the home his mother had been renting for the past 12 years. Neither was the money considered for the padding of a nest egg.

The story above illustrates how a person's income is NOT always a measure of financial security. There are many people who fall into the trap of thinking that marrying someone with a high paying job means they're going to be better off financially. THIS IS NOT TRUE! Sometimes, a person with a high income and higher spending habits can put us in more debt than we could ever imagine. A six-figure doctor may be inclined to feel that because his income is so high, he can afford a higher debt level than most Americans. This kind of flawed thinking enters into nearly every American family.

After you've spent some time observing your mate, you probably want to discuss their feelings about their own family members. This is a sensitive subject, so make sure you tread carefully. It's not a matter of interrogating them, you simply want to feel them out:

- Do they perceive their financial choices with indifference, or do they somehow feel the need to save the world?

- Can their parents make the mortgage on their own, or do they guilt trip their children into saving them financially?

- How financially stable are the other siblings?

- If there is a financial crisis, does most of the burden fall onto one person, or is it shared equally?

- If financial burdens are shared equally among the children, does every child usually participate, or only the more responsible children?

- What about the extended family? Is your partner's nuclear family closely connected to the extended family or distinct? Does your partner's nuclear family feel the need to participate in solving problems created by the extended family?

The point is this: you should have a full and complete understanding of anyone and anything that lies within the sphere of influence of your partner. This is not snooping. It's looking out for the interests of yourself and your family. You will never know everything of course, but that doesn't mean you shouldn't try.

If you do your analysis and don't like what you see, it doesn't mean you should dump your partner. Love is not so cheap as to be discarded over something like money (well, it sometimes depends on *how much money* we're talking about). Your response to the situations above may depend on how your partner is handling it.

I would argue that if you feel your partner has created sufficient distance between himself/herself and "problem relatives", then there is no issue to be resolved. What's also important is that you spend more time trusting your instincts than believing every word someone says. There may also be cases in which your mere disagreement with the way the family handles money can cause problems in your relationship. Remember: there is probably nothing abnormal in your partner's mind about how his/her family handles money and deals with one another. As far as your partner knows, this is how a family is SUPPOSED to behave. Expressing problems you see with your partner's family structure can lead to angry, defensive behavior. It can also cause huge problems in the long-run with in-laws who feel that you have somehow stolen away their relative, or that you're prying into their personal affairs.

With all this said, I recommend that you observe, engage in minimal discussion, and then make a set of decisions. If it's necessary for you to share your thoughts and plan of action with your partner, then do so. But understand that there may be times when you simply must act now and discuss later.

Martha saw the horrible habits of her in-laws, and this concerned her. She saw that Jerry's family lived a life of financial insecurity, drifting from one crisis to another as a result of poor financial planning. Their fly-by-night approach to life was not the kind of life she wanted to live.

She talked to Jerry about it, simply asking him if he felt that there was anything wrong with the way his family handled money. Initially, Jerry was not sure what she was referring to. "We like to show our love at Christmas", he responded, minimizing the problem. But after some discussion, he admitted that there was a problem with the way his family handled money. He expressed a deep seated emotion that has stayed with him since childhood. He recalled having to hide from the landlord when the rent was due, and not having enough food in the house when his father would spend his entire salary at the casino. All of this bothered him, and it was not until his conversation with Martha that he realized that some degree of change was necessary.

As a result, he agreed to give less money to his sister than usual (as she consistently seemed "tapped out" at the end of the month). He also agreed that he would talk with other relatives about ways to share the rent when his mother could not pay what she owed the landlord. They also agreed that when they were married, they would move to Oregon, creating some distance between he and his family.

This outcome satisfied Martha, but she was still worried. She saw how close Jerry was with his family and wasn't sure what to believe when it came to the changes he had promised. Concerned about her own financial security, she also took personal steps to insulate herself from the rest of Jerry's family. First, they agreed that they would not share checking accounts. They would have one joint account which would be used ONLY for paying bills, another small joint investment account, and the rest of their income would be their own. She knew that Jerry was not likely to save much of his money, so she knew that she would be the one to incur the bulk of the responsibility when it came to saving money. She also knew that she would have to hide some money from Jerry. Well, not really hide it, but keep it tied up in some illiquid assets to make it more difficult for him to borrow from her. By "illiquid", we are referring to real estate, investment art, a small business, or some other place where money is put but can't be easily turned back into cash. That way, if he asked to use her money, she could honestly say that she didn't have any. You could say that she was being a little dishonest so that she could be more honest later on. So, Martha expanded her dog grooming business, which eventually ate into her personal investment funds. This not only allowed her to save money, but it also protected her from her husband and his borrowing relatives.

Martha's approach might be deemed deceptive, but the reality that she's confronted with is the fact that marriage is a PARTNERSHIP, and sometimes, we must protect ourselves from weaknesses in the partnership. It's as simple as that.

Other things you might want to consider doing to protect yourself from bad relatives:

1) Agree in writing that you and your partner must agree on any decision to loan money to a relative.

The LAST thing you want is for your partner to come home and say "I just gave $1,000 to Rick and the kids." This isn't fair to you, and if you do not set a precedent early, these issues may haunt you throughout your relationship.

2) ***Keep separate accounts for yourselves***

Sometimes having your own money and having your partner have their own money is a good way to allow everyone to do what he or she wants. If you think that your partner isn't going to save any of the money from their own account, you may want to consider a joint savings account where both partners contribute, and neither partner can get access to the funds without the other partner's signature.

3) ***Consider distancing yourselves from relatives that might cause the most financial trouble.***

Distance can be a wonderful thing. It's not as if you are keeping your mate away from their loved ones, but it helps you to develop your own identity as a couple. Also, it's much easier to remain disconnected from financial and other family drama if you're not right down the street. Out of sight can mean out of mind, take it from someone with experience!

4) ***Don't flaunt your wealth around relatives***

One good way to keep someone from borrowing money from you is to borrow from them first. While you may not want to take this approach, you'll get a feel for what approach works best around the relatives most likely to borrow money. An absolute no-no is to show up to every family gathering with status symbols, nice new clothes for the kids, and money falling out of your pocket. The reality is that human beings are ultimately "human", and some scientists even argue that human beings are simply intelligent animals (At the very least, it can be argued that we all have very strong animal instincts). Every animal wants access to resources for survival. When another human is lacking the resources they need, and you appear to have an abundance of resources, you *cannot blame them for seeking out the resources from you.* So, if you ensure that they are unaware of what you have, then you avoid that problem altogether.

5) Tie up your monthly incomes by: paying bills, making investments or reaching firm financial goals (saving for a home, buying investment property, accumulating funds in your savings account, etc.)

If you account for every single penny, then there isn't as much money to waste. You may need to do this in order to create convenient excuses for why you can't help relatives.

6) Create a budget for "helping others" with your partner to give them some latitude to help those he/she loves.

If you and your partner are extremely loyal to other members of the family, there are times when you must simply accept the fact that you're going to have to help others outside of your nuclear family. This isn't a crime and it doesn't lead to financial destruction. You can budget funds each month to create a "good will fund". In this fund, you can have money just sitting there in case someone comes along with an emergency. This shows that you are good people without breaking the bank in the process.

7) If you expect that parents will be living with you in the future, make plans for that circumstance.

There's nothing wrong with having relatives live with you, it happens all the time. Proper financial planning can prepare you for this possibility. If given enough time and planning, perhaps you can save your money to eventually buy a home with a mother-in-law suite or large basement. You may even want to call on the resources of other relatives to help you plan for this. If you decide that either your parents or your in-laws will eventually reside in a nursing home, plan for this as well.

Senior citizens aren't helpless. Most of them have some form of income, and some have accumulated financial assets throughout their lives. So having a retired person live with you can actually benefit everyone. In your long-term planning, you may want to persuade the parent to pay down the mortgage on their home so they can contribute home equity to their long-term care. This means that they will have wealth accumulated in the value of their home and may be eligible for bank loans or other sources of financing to contribute to the cost of taking care of them. Your senior will appreciate the fact that you're giving them the opportunity to earn their keep, since most people don't want to be a burden on others. Additionally, you may think of other ways they can contribute to the family, such as saving you money on a sitter or helping with the house cleaning. There is always something that someone else can contribute if he/she has the right attitude.

8) *Be careful what you volunteer for*

If you are the first to step up and volunteer whenever someone in the family has a financial problem, then you have effectively designated yourself as the family subsidizer. People will not only expect your help when you offer it; they're going to expect your help *whenever* there is a financial problem. Understand that people are watching, and others learn how to treat you by how you tell them to treat you.

- What is going to happen to her parents when they get old? Has the family discussed this yet? Are they willing to?

- Does your partner have any problems with the way you interact with your own family members?

- If he were to get a raise, does he feel that it should be public information (meaning, does he tell everyone or just you)? If he buys a house for a certain price, do others have the right to know how much has been paid for it?

- How did the family go about resolving their last two or three financial crises?

- Are his or her parents relatively independent or do they depend on the resources of others in the family?

- If he goes to dinner with his family, who pays the bill?

Answering these questions, plus any others that come up can help you both get a clearer picture of what you're dealing with. It can also help each of you plan how you're going to manage your finances together in the future. I'm not telling you how you should react to this information, just that it should at least be discussed.

AVOIDING A FINANCIAL VENEREAL DISEASE

More women than men in committed relationships (33% vs. 26%) have not been completely honest to their spouses or partners about their spending habits[18]

[18] http://family-law.lawyers.com/Stats-and-Facts-Love-and-Money.html

Yes, it sounds gross, but the reality is that you may run into someone who carries a "Financial V.D.". What kind of person carries such a disease? Someone who has engaged in a series of bad choices that will serve to infect your otherwise healthy financial situation. The thing about Venereal Diseases, financial or otherwise, is that they are not uniform. There are a multitude of ways that someone can catch a disease, and quite a few symptoms. Additionally, there are a large number of possible consequences for merging with someone who has this problem. You shouldn't assume that just because you are diseased that it's ok to merge with someone else who is diseased. Sexually, if you have gonoreah, and someone else has herpes, is that a good combination? No! You're both going to end up as two people with both diseases at the same time. *My point is that diseases don't cancel each other out and neither do bad financial choices.* Don't believe that because you have engaged in bad choices yourself that you deserve to be with someone else who has also made bad choices. That choice, in itself, is a bad one.

Many of the rules of thumb for financial VD are very similar to the rules when it comes to regular VD:

1) You can't judge a book by its cover
2) Many people aren't going to be honest about their situation.
3) Diseases and treatment can be costly.
4) There are many ways to protect yourself from an infected partner.
5) The burden of the disease will become yours if you tie yourself to that person.

It's very easy for a person to hide financial problems. He can hide it through status symbols, or use the fact that people often assume that a person with a high income is financially healthy. What's sad is that many of the BMWs we see on the street are owned by people who can barely afford the payments. Many of the nice homes people live in are mortgaged to the bone. Even homes that have appreciated in value can be over-mortgaged to the point that the owner owns almost nothing.

Therefore, you shouldn't presume that simply because someone appears to be doing well, he actually is. In our society, there's incredible pressure to "keep up with the people down the street", which leads to many people spending beyond their means. Effectively, they end up giving up their future in favor of the present. In some ways, this has become "The American Way".

Remember: you're merging financial bodies with someone, and if your partner's body is not healthy, then yours won't be either. Many people don't think about these issues when they fall in love, but after the reality of the relationship sets in, they realize that they could've fallen in love with someone who didn't pose such a great financial burden.

When it comes to Financial VD, people are not always going to openly admit their problems. You're going to have to be the doctor, paying attention to the symptoms, and ultimately, making a diagnosis. So spend time observing, thinking and paying attention to the information your partner releases, and you'll eventually have an idea of where he/she stands.

I am going to list some types of Financial VD, along with a description of the symptoms. Perhaps you can identify these attributes in your partner, or maybe even yourself.

Types of Financial Venereal Diseases that your partner may carry:

1) POOR SPENDING AND SAVING HABITS

Bad spending habits are similar to smoking. Years of smoking may have done damage already, but the greatest damage is going to occur over the next 50 years. Although a person may seem relatively healthy today, in a few decades, she or he may be a prime candidate for lung cancer.

The primary symptom of poor spending habits is that a person could probably not survive very long if he were to lose his job. I've seen people with six figure and even seven figure incomes who literally live from paycheck to paycheck. While this person's income level may lead others to conclude that he is financially secure, the reality is that he is financially insecure.

To diagnose this disease, you should pay attention to your partner's spending habits. Do his spending habits change as he gets closer to payday? Does he talk more about what he's spending money on than about what he is saving to purchase later? Does he ever discuss financial investments he's made? The answers to these questions will tell you if you are dealing with someone with a spending or saving VD. I won't discuss saving VDs separately, since spending and saving are closely connected. If you are not saving, it's probably because you are spending, and if you are not spending, it is easier to save.

2) A PATHETIC CREDIT HISTORY

A poor credit history can be debilitating to a family. If one partner has maintained stellar credit, while the other has destroyed his or her credit, then there's going to be a tough road ahead for this family as they attempt to purchase a home, a car or any other big ticket item requiring them to borrow money. If the family can get a loan, there is the additional burden of high interest rates plaguing the family.

The other problem with credit history is that it's tough to observe. Many times, a partner with poor credit is not likely to tell the world that their credit stinks. This is where you really have to put on your physician's hat and pay close attention.

The best way to find out if your partner has poor credit is to simply ask her about her credit score. You may not want to ask directly, but a simple question like "My credit score went down when I tried to (fill in the blank). Have you ever had this problem?" Just getting your partner to talk about credit is a good way to get her to spill the beans.

Chances are that if your partner has no idea what his credit score is, and if he does not check it regularly, he probably doesn't have an incredibly high score. A high credit score is something that takes some work and focus to create, and most high scores are not created by accident.

Pay attention to whether or not your partner pays their bills on time. If you notice that things are paid late, or that your partner has defaulted on a car loan or other personal loans, chances are that his credit score is not very good.

You may also want to talk about your partner's past. If he mentions that he's filed bankruptcy or had financial problems in the past, this is another negative sign. None of these things imply for sure that his rating is horrible, but these issues can be symptoms of a larger problem.

3) HORRIFIC DEBT LEVELS

Debt is one of the great burdens of American society. Regular people have it. Our government has it. It seems that nowadays, debt is the way to get what you want. It allows us to live well today off of money we don't even have yet. In some ways, it presents an amazing opportunity. At the same time, it can be a crippling burden as we try to make ourselves financially solvent.

As I noted earlier in the book, the WORST kind of debt to have is credit card debt, especially if there's nothing to show for it. Excessive credit card debt may indicate that your mate has a spending problem. Spending problems don't just go away, so you may end up battling debt problems of the past, while incurring additional debt in the future.

There are many ways you can tell if your partner has a lot of debt. One indication is how many credit cards your partner has, and how often he uses them. The more credit cards your partner has, the more debt he's likely to have. If he does not explicitly state that the balance is paid off every month, chances are the debt burden is enormous.

Another type of "bad debt" is car loan debt. Cars depreciate in value, so many people are paying for years on an asset that has a value below the amount owed on the loan. Creating large amounts of auto debt is not only crippling, but it also can reflect poor decision making. One way to determine if your partner has a great deal of auto loan debt is to ask how high his/her car payments are, and when the purchase was made. If the purchase was recent and the payments are high, chances are that your partner will bring some auto debt into the relationship.

A type of "good debt" is student loan debt or debt on a mortgage. While these types of debt can be good, they can also be tough to manage. This is especially true if your partner has taken out home equity loans (loans that use the borrower's home equity as collateral). So the fact that the home has a high value, coupled with the fact that your partner has made continuous payments does not necessarily imply that your partner has a great deal of equity. Equity represents the percentage of the home your mate actually owns, as opposed to the debt owed for the money borrowed to buy the house.

When it comes to loans taken out for educational purposes, I consider this to be a good use of debt. However, there are some who borrow large sums without going into a field paying a high enough salary to manage their debt. For example, you may be dating a person with a Ph.D. in English who borrowed over $100,000 in order to get there. This can be difficult to manage, since English Ph.D.s don't usually have very high salaries. Your partner might be able to correct your grammar, but he may not be able to bring home the bacon if you like to eat pork (of course this is not meant to condemn English Ph.D.s, who can sometimes earn large sums of money).

A candid conversation with your partner about debt is not unreasonable, since your partner's debt is going to affect you. I recommend asking your partner directly about his debt levels, giving him the opportunity to share this information with you.

4) COSTLY AND DESTRUCTIVE PERSONAL HABITS

Destructive personal habits represent one of the worst kinds of Financial VD, because they can be so horribly devastating. When I say "costly personal habits", I am referring to things like gambling, drugs, or even things patronizing prostitutes. These habits are difficult to diagnose, since many people don't disclose their habits to others, especially those who are closest to them. These habits can bring shame, particularly to those who have distinguished positions in the community.

The diagnosis of these habits tends to rely a great deal on the use of your gut instincts. While someone will almost never admit that he spends money on drugs, you can pick-up on this habit after spending some time with the person. If you are also involved in drugs, this is multiplying one bad habit with another, leading to sure financial ruin for yourself and your family.

I have seen entire families ruined by gambling problems. This is a tough illness to fight and diagnose, and many people affected by it don't admit that they have a problem. What's worse is that the person usually minimizes the depth of the problem, and their partner does not find out how bad things are until it's too late. If your partner loves to gamble, take all the steps necessary to protect yourself. I also recommend not necessarily taking their word for it when it comes to describing how bad the problem is. Go with your instincts. Few gambling addicts are going to invite the ostracism that comes with admitting that they have such a destructive habit.

To avoid the ostracism, an addict will either lie to you, lie to himself, or both.

The additional burden of such costly habits is that they can lead not only to financial ruin, but to legal problems as well. Many people have gone to prison for tax evasion resulting from a gambling or drug problem. Unless you have a desire to enter into such a lifestyle, pay close attention to your partner's habits, or else you may be the one who pays the price.

5) UNDISCLOSED FINANCIAL OBLIGATIONS

Undisclosed financial obligations is a sticky disease in which someone hides important information from you, such as a pending lawsuit, child support obligations or something else that will cause her long-term financial hardship. It's tough to diagnose and can be crippling to your financial future.

Listen to your partner. Observe his or her life as if it were your own, because one day, your partner's life will be your own. This is the best way to diagnose potential problems with Financial VD.

Treatment Options for Financial VD

If you find that your love for your partner is so great that you are willing to work through his or her financial VD, then I congratulate you. You must be in love, and this must mean that you believe this person is well-worth the fight. That's nothing to be ashamed of, since we all have flaws. The ultimate question to ask is whether the person you love is worth the trouble. Let's assume your partner IS worth it. How do you live with Financial VD?

Here are some treatment options you might want to consider:

1) Changing of spending habits

If you or your partner's venereal disease is poor spending and/or savings habits, then a change in behavior is critical. As I've reiterated many times throughout this book, good money management is more about habits and personality than know-how. You can be a financial wizard, but if you don't know how to save and manage your cash, you will always end up in the poor house.

If you find that your partner has habits that can be detrimental to your financial future, you should discuss the problem, suggest a solution, and then watch to see if there is a change in behavior. Many people are reluctant to change, since old habits die hard. If you are not happy with the change you are seeing or not seeing before tying the knot, then you probably shouldn't tie the knot at all. At the very least, if you do so, then you are doing so at your own risk.

If you find that your partner is receptive to your suggestions, then sit down and make a plan. Try to track down the specific behavior leading to the problem, and then correct it. It may mean that you or your partner should stop using credit cards so much, or that she should put cash in his savings and investments before he begins spending. Be gentle, since the fix is probably an easy one, requiring only modest behavioral modifications. Also, remember that poor habits took time to form, so they'll take time to break. Small changes practiced over time can go a long way.

2) Going through the credit repair process

There are credit repair services in existence which can help you get back on your financial feet. DO NOT pay for services that tell you they can fix your credit report in a short period of time! There is no substitute for time when it comes to credit repair. However, there are companies designed for credit counseling that can be of help, and many of them are free.

Be extremely careful with these companies. Many of them were subject to IRS investigations due to the fact that they were accused of preying on debt-ridden consumers. When choosing a company to help with credit repair, there are some red flags you should avoid to help you distinguish the good from the bad.

- *How high are the fees?* If the fees are outrageous, chances are the company is trying to get over on you. You shouldn't pay more than $100 dollars per month for most debt management programs. At the very least, you should shop around for the best company, checking with at least five services before making a decision. If you find five "clean" services (ones that fit this check list), compare those five and then make a decision.

- *Does the company provide consumer counseling and education, or does it just spit out a debt management program in ten minutes?* If the approach is too quick, chances are that it's not customized. A good credit repair company is going to spend time with you to work on your particular situation. It will also provide on-going counseling to help your long-term financial future.

- *Is the agency accredited?* Does the company have complaints filed against them from other consumers? It's best to work with credit counseling services that are accredited by the National Foundation for Credit Counseling (800-388-2227) or the Association of Independent Consumer Credit Counseling Services (800-450-1794). You can also check with the Better Business Bureau or your state's Attorney General's Office in order to find out if the company has had any complaints filed against it.

While working with a credit counseling agency, you should not take on any new debt. That means you should STOP using your credit cards, and delay the purchase of any items that you cannot purchase with cash. The only way for you to move forward financially is to stop moving backward.

For more information on credit counseling, go to the National Foundation for Consumer Credit's website: www.nfcc.org.

3) Set goals and plans for getting out of debt

When you talk to your sweetie about the debt problem, set goals together. I recommend setting financial goals, since Financial Lovemaking involves sharing mutual fantasies. Once you set your goals, you can design strategies to reach them. These strategies are going to involve changing little habits in order to work together as a couple toward your financial security. You might be able to save money on things you do together. For example, you might decide that "We are only going to go out to dinner once a week." This can be your first step toward becoming a financial union. Other tips are listed below:

- Renting movies instead of going to the movies
- Exhausting all free options before doing things that cost money (How about keeping a long list of free stuff that you can do that can be done long before you start doing things that cost money?)

- Going out on dates with no credit cards and only a fixed amount of cash in your pocket.
- Cutting down on the number of visits you make to expensive night clubs.
- Having more gatherings with other couples (since personalized gatherings at home are usually low cost).
- Going on drives through the country or checking out local parks.
- Creating a free surprise for each other once every two weeks.

There are a tremendous number of ways that you can get out of debt, save money and fall in love, all at the same time. Think hard, and you can find your way to a more exciting, more creative and less expensive relationship.

4) Wearing a Financial Condom

If you find that your partner is not willing to change any of his/her personal habits, then you might need to protect yourself. When I use the term "Financial VD", I'm referring not only to an individual's current financial health, but also to their habits. If someone is financially sick, he can usually get better by making the right choices. But there are times when someone is financially sick and does not view it as a problem. Some people don't want to start a financially healthy lifestyle. Instead, anyone with the misfortune of crossing their path is going to find himself being victimized by this person's negative choices.

In the face of Financial VD, the best way to become financially protected is to find a different partner. But if you either feel that the problems are not harmful enough to warrant leaving the relationship, or you simply love the person so much that you can't let him or her go, then there are ways you can at least minimize the damage. I call these "financial condoms" since they allow you to interact with someone without catching whatever disease they are carrying. Want to try on a financial condom for size? Well, here is what you might want to do:

Create separate bank accounts and separate credit cards

Rule number 1 for dealing with someone with financial VD is to not mix your money with theirs. If he/she is overspending and under-saving, then the merging of your money with their own is only going to enable unhealthy behavior. Before long, your money will also belong to the local shopping mall, and you'll feel like you've been taken for a ride.

This is especially true for credit cards. Credit cards are easy sources of money, and if both of your names are on the card, it's not very difficult for the person to apply for credit increases or other things that can destroy you financially. The sad thing is that if you are merging your finances with someone who has no financial discipline, all of your hard work is going to go down the drain. I have seen couples where one spouse works hard to save, while the other spouse has charged $10,000 dollars in credit card debt without the other spouse's knowledge. If your partner is not on the same page with you, then don't allow them access to ANYTHING you own financially.

Separate names on EVERYTHING!

If you buy a car, get it in your own name. If you buy a home together, make sure your name is on the deed. If you buy anything that requires fixed payments, and it belongs to you,

you should get it solely in your own name. If your partner's the one who wants to make the purchase, then he should get it in his own name. This way, if he fails to make the payments, you can try to argue that the debt should be his financial responsibility. By at least trying to keep things financially separate, you may be able to get away from these debts in the event of a divorce.

The thing is that if you are financially responsible, this gives someone else the opportunity to prey on you. He/she can prey on your good credit, and this person can prey on your financial capacity. This is bad news, and you shouldn't fall into this trap. The same thing applies for co-signing on loans....don't do it!

Taxes represent another potential danger of Financial Lovemaking. If the IRS sees a problem with one partner's income, they're likely to come after you both. So, if your mate has gambling income he doesn't report, drug spending/proceeds or other areas of financial irresponsibility, this can come back to haunt you. Given that the IRS shows no mercy, I recommend not filing joint taxes with someone who can get you into trouble.

If your mate enjoys spending, let her do it all

If you have a partner who loves to spend, and she can afford to do it, then you may want to just let them do it (with her own money, of course). This can lead to a silent splitting of responsibilities, as you become the saver, and she becomes the spender. If you go out to dinner and they want to spend, let them pay for it. If they want a big screen TV and you don't, let them pay for it. Contribute if you feel it's necessary, but sometimes, spending is an addiction, and if you must allow them to feed their addiction, at least allow them to do so in a way that is going to help both of you. This holds especially true if your partner earns a great deal more than you. A higher income may make your partner feel as if it's her responsibility to make the bulk of the purchases. If that's the case, then that's okay. By doing most of the saving for the family, you are working together to achieve financial security and also enjoying the positive effects of prosperity.

Keep both eyes on all financial ventures and accounts

I have a saying: "In any relationship, silent partners do not get to make financial love. Silent partners simply get screwed". Yes, that statement might be a bit crass to some, but it's not nearly as crass as having someone take advantage of you. The damage can be devastating and last a lifetime.

If you're merging your finances with a poor spender and saver, you have to keep both eyes on your financial accounts at all times. Don't allow someone who is not financially responsible to take responsibility for your money! This is a recipe for disaster. I have seen this problem mostly with women dealing with men who feel that their manhood dictates that they should be responsible for all family financial decisions. Effectively, their lack of empowerment leads them down a path toward financial ruin.

Be informed of *everything* going on in your financial life, and all joint accounts you have with your partner. Check them regularly. You may want to ensure that any account owned by both of you requires the signature of both parties for any transactions to commence. If your partner has one of the financial illnesses mentioned above, you may wake up one day to find that the account you've been building for years has been reduced to nothing. This is a HORRIBLE feeling.

Use budgets and prearrangements on spending

Sometimes the best way to get someone to slow their spending is to allow him/her to spend….within limits. I've always argued that for most Americans, the reasons we are overweight and broke are not because we eat and spend. It's because we eat and spend WITHOUT MODERATION. So, if you are dealing with a spendaholic, the crime may not be in the activity itself. Instead, it's because the person does not know when to stop spending. She goes to the mall and shops till she drops, rather than shopping until she has what she needs. He goes to the casino and spends every penny in his bank account, rather than simply spend all the money in his pocket. This is what gets people into financial trouble.

I recommend that when it comes to your loved one, simply work with him or her on whatever habit he or she has that's financially detrimental, and find ways to budget room for their financial choices. Give him money to go shopping or even to gamble, but set limits. Make the implicit agreement that no credit cards are to be available during this activity, and that once the cash in their pocket is gone, he has to go home. This can work for some, although people with serious problems may not agree with this approach. If that's the case, then go back to the earlier rules (financial condoms), and keep your own money at a distance. You can't always control what others are doing, but you can control the choices you make yourself.

Do not play the role of an enabler

Even if your partner insists upon continuing with his poor financial habits, you don't have to remain silent about it. Make it clear that you don't approve of these choices, and don't allow yourself to silently approve these choices by playing a role in them. If your partner loves to gamble, don't go with him. If she wants to use drugs, don't spend time around her when she is doing it. Silently supporting your partner's poor financial habits is no different from enjoying a cheeseburger with your overweight sibling every time he gets hungry. Even if there is no immediate change in behavior resulting from your statements, your partner is certainly taking note of your disapproval. If he loves you, he will modify his behavior, or at least control it as much as possible.

Does it make sense to consider hiding your assets?

I am not one to encourage or discourage the act of keeping some of your assets out of your partner's view, but I can say that it's done all the time. There are some partners who, for whatever reason, feel compelled to keep money aside that their mate doesn't know about. Not to say that I recommend doing this sort of thing, I am only saying that people do it.

I would only consider engaging in this kind of behavior if you have serious reason to believe that your partner is going to be financially irresponsible. However, this can come back to haunt you in the event of divorce. Also, if you are forced to be deceptive with your partner, then it might be time to consider being with someone else. Little white lies are one thing, but major lies are another.

5) Getting treatment for social disorders

Some of the financial venereal diseases mentioned above are more serious than others. Being a spendaholic is not as bad as being a thief, and being a non-saver is not as bad as using drugs or gambling. It's important that you always remain aware of the seriousness of bad personal habits, even if they initially seem harmless. Such habits ruin families every day, and cause untold financial devastation. You should protect yourself in every way possible, no matter what it takes.

Given that you have the love and patience to go through the process, you may want to demand that your partner seek help for whatever problem is plaguing him. I again recommend going with your gut when it comes to determining if your mate has a problem. If you feel that he drinks too much, then go ahead and presume that he has a drinking problem. If he's going to the casino on a regular basis, then this may be work for Gamblers Anonymous. The key is not to address the problem AFTER it's gotten out of control. You want to attack the issue before it becomes a problem.

6) Prenuptial agreements

The prenuptial agreement is the ultimate financial condom. Many people consider prenuptial agreements to be tools of the rich, but that's not the case. A person with few assets can use a prenuptial agreement to protect what he/she has, and the tool is just as effective.

What is a "prenup" (short for prenuptial agreement)? It's an agreement between two parties that details how assets will be split in the event of a divorce. Over half of all couples end their marriages in divorce, so even if you don't think you are on the bad half of things, you may still want to be prepared. Some consider a prenup to be a violation of the love and trust you have for one another. In reality, it can be considered a form of insurance, or even better, a chance to show your love to your partner through "optimal contracting". Optimal contracting simply means that you do whatever you can in advance to avoid misunderstanding in the future which can further destroy a relationship. By creating a prenup, you are saying to your partner "I believe things are going to work out. But if they don't, I don't want to allow further destruction of the love and respect we have for one another by creating financial confusion." Perhaps you may buy this argument, perhaps not. Either way, you may want to consider using a prenuptial agreement.

When might you use a prenup?

- If you have a lump sum of cash or assets you want to protect.
- If you own a business.
- If you expect to receive an inheritance from a relative.
- If you have children from a prior marriage that you wish to protect financially.
- You're going to see a big increase in income from a business venture or achieving a degree in a high paying profession.
- If you want your divorce to go as smoothly as possible (Messy divorces are both emotionally and financially draining, and can scar you for life).

If you discuss the issue, I recommend touching on it as early as possible. That way, the person knows where you stand long before you have fallen in love. Also, you may want to highlight how your partner can benefit from such an agreement. If there are no apparent benefits, then tell him that you or your family may feel more comfortable with him if he signs the agreement. This may or may not be true, but it could work.

Sit together and make a loose agreement with your partner about what you have, and how you would each like to distribute it in the event of divorce. Then, you should see an attorney. Not consulting an attorney with a prenup can get it thrown out in court. So you should be willing to spend the extra money on the agreement. Hire separate attorneys, since using the same lawyer can cause problems with enforcement of the contract. Separate attorneys will allow both your interests to be represented fully.

To make the agreement valid, make sure that you sign it well in advance of the wedding. Presenting the agreement shortly before the wedding may cause the courts to believe that you coerced your mate into signing the contract, which makes it invalid. At least two months before the wedding is a safe period to review and ratify the agreement.

Be honest about what you have, ensuring that each party fully discloses all financial assets. If you hide anything, all bets are off. Be generous with the way assets are divided. If the agreement leaves your partner in financial ruin, many courts are going to throw it out. This doesn't mean that you give your partner everything, but perhaps leaving him/her with 10 – 20% of your assets might be fair. After all, you DO love him, right?

Don't make agreements on things that don't involve money, except in rare situations. It might be nice to say that your partner has to have sex with you once a week, but that isn't going to fly in court. On a more serious note, enclosing things like the number of times he should call you or whether he must keep a job aren't usually going to be upheld in court.

Prenuptial agreements cannot free you from things like child support payments, so get that out of your head right now. The children have nothing to do with the agreement, so they aren't affected by it, at least not directly. Keep the agreement updated, at least every five to ten years, as your circumstances change. You can also create postnuptial agreements, which are written after the marriage has taken place.

Some states are "Equitable Distribution States", where all marital property is shared equally. But, most states don't have this requirement. Therefore, if you make arrangements in advance, chances are your arrangements will be supported in the court of law. Do research on your home state to find out the specifics.

The point of this chapter is to encourage you to feel the freedom to make proper choices when it comes to how you're affected by the financial choices of your partner. Be smart when dealing with those who can affect your life, don't rely on random chance to determine whether you'll be financially secure. Remember: *Loving* together means *living* together, and *having* together means *giving* together. If you and your mate are on the same page, then Financial Lovemaking can be a wonderful process!

36361649R00127

Made in the USA
San Bernardino, CA
20 July 2016